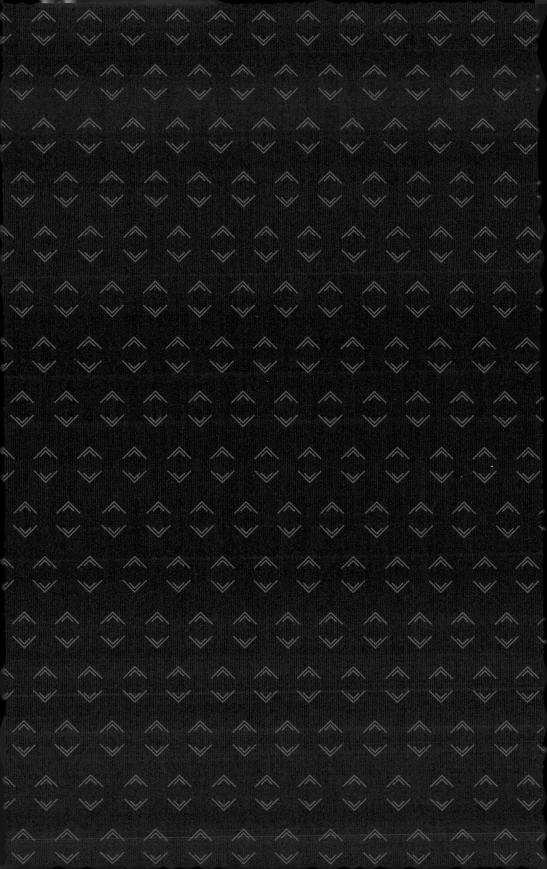

The
4 WILLS
of
GOD

The
4 WILLS
of
GOD

*The Way He Directs Our Steps
and Frees Us to Direct Our Own*

Dr. Emerson
Eggerichs

PUBLISHING GROUP

NASHVILLE, TENNESSEE

978-1-4627-4373-5

Published by B&H Publishing Group
Nashville, Tennessee

Dewey Decimal Classification: 231.5
Subject Heading: GOD-WILL \ PROVIDENCE AND
GOVERNMENT OF GOD \ CHRISTIAN LIFE

1 2 3 4 5 6 7 • 22 21 20 19 18

To my daughter Joy Eggerichs Reed for her belief in this message and determination to make sure it went to print—after the manuscript sat on the shelf for many years—so that others could be blessed by the message in the way God blessed her through His four wills. Her vision to broadcast this biblical revelation has humbled and honored me.

CONTENTS

Introduction
"START HERE!"

You will not be surprised to learn that everyone asks the same question when I share that God has four wills.

"What are these four wills?"

I state:

> Believe in Jesus Christ (John 6:40)
>
> Abstain from Sexual Sin (1 Thessalonians 4:3)
>
> Give Thanks in Everything (1 Thessalonians 5:18)
>
> Submit in Doing Right (1 Peter 2:13–15)

Each of these is declared to be the will of God.

> In John 6:40 Jesus said, "This is the will of My Father."
>
> In 1 Thessalonians 4:3 Paul states, "For this is the will of God."
>
> In 1 Thessalonians 5:18 the apostle pens, "this is God's will for you."
>
> In 1 Peter 2:15 Peter writes, "For such is the will of God."

These four stand out from all other Bible verses because each distinctly identifies God's will.

Though there is more to God's will than these four, if we ignore these four wills—unmistakably highlighted—it is questionable that we will follow the other commands of God.

For this reason, I urge every believer, young or old, to "Start Here!"

I do. Again and again.

I first learned of these four wills in my twenties. Pastor John MacArthur published a book on the will of God. He shared that he found these in a book called the *Treasury of Scriptural Knowledge*. From there, I tracked down these same findings. Now, after decades of studying the Bible and counseling others, I can say firmly that these foundational commands of Christ and the apostles serve as a life compass.

As I look back over my life, decisions made at the major crossroads of my life were made in response to the principles of the four wills. Though I was not aware of what I refer to now as the B.A.G.S. acronym (Believe, Abstain, Give Thanks, Submit), in hindsight, I can see that these four commands served as pivotal markers. When I carried this godly "baggage," noteworthy events ensued! Following them led me forward through confusing, trying, and rewarding moments. Sometimes the four wills positioned me to experience God's favor. At other times, they revealed shortcomings before I got derailed and lost communion with God. But, they always mattered. Like the four points on a compass, they helped me chart my life course. As a checklist, they served me well in doing and determining God's will.

Actually, there are two profound ways these four wills have served as a map. The subtitle to this book is "The Way God Directs Our Steps and Frees Us to Direct Our Own." This book is about the two wonderful experiences that can result when each of us follow these four wills.

Result #1

God uniquely leads us when we follow these four wills. He directs our individual steps. He guides us as we trust and obey Him. He opens doors that are distinct to us. There is a triggering effect. As I say, "Follow His four universal wills and experience His unique will for your life."

Result #2

When we follow these four wills, yet God does not seem to uniquely direct our steps, we are free to direct our own steps. We can decide for ourselves. We can do what we wish based on what seems good and best. We are permitted to do this because in following the four wills, we are near the center of God's will, and these serve as guardrails against sinful choices.

Why Did You Pick Up This Book?

But let's back up to where you might be right now in your journey. If you are like most of us, you are asking, "How can I discover God's will for my life?" Is that not why you picked up this book to read?

Upon reflection, isn't it the most significant question a person can ask? If there is a God who loves us and has a purpose for us then finding His unique will surfaces to the top as one of the most important things we can do. All of us should ask, "What is God's personal purpose for my life?"

But when this question is asked, I tenderly counter, should we be asking "What is God's will for my life?" or should we be asking, "What is God's will?"

The secret I unfold in this book is that the answer to "What is God's will for my life?" is found after we answer, "What is God's will?"

The freeing news is that if we do not receive an answer to "What is God's will for my life?" we will still be okay. We are doing the four universal wills of God. This is God's will for our life! We win either way.

However, these four are not always easy to do.

Who wants to identify with Jesus Christ in a hostile environment when it is easier to deny knowing Him and thereby enjoy acceptance and approval from the world?

Who wants to give thanks when bad things are happening and it is easier to be angry and resentful over the injustices?

Who wants to abstain from sex when it is easier to yield to our sensual cravings or yield to a culture that demands you live together first before marriage because to the secular society abstaining before marriage is antiquated and unrealistic?

Who wants to submit in doing what is right, especially to authority figures who are unreasonable, when it is easier to do wrong and gain from the
wrong?

There is a price to pay.

But as I will unfold in this book, that is a small price to pay for receiving
God's kind guidance and peaceful presence. We actually get to "see" the hand
of the Creator of the Universe, a cosmos that is expansive, boundless, immeasurable, limitless, and infinite, show up in our tiny lives. Our minds should
be boggled at how much we matter to Him and by His personal response to
us. As Jesus said, "seek first His kingdom and His righteousness, and all these
things will be added to you" (Matthew 6:33). God enters our world by meeting our essential needs, and possibly more (Mark 10:29–30), as we pursue
His revelation and purpose.

In this book, I tell story after story of how our loving heavenly Father
shows up, how He Himself adds to our lives. For Him, it isn't about time,
space, or matter. For Him, it is about relationship. What is most significant to Him is our heart for Him, and for us to discover His heart for us.
Encouragingly, as we follow His four wills, we reveal our heart to Him and
discover His heart for us.

As long as we are believing in Jesus Christ, abstaining from sexual sin,
giving thanks in everything, and submitting in doing right (B.A.G.S.), God
will uniquely respond to us. We will have touched and warmed His heart.
And, when He does not direct our steps as we hoped and prayed, we can
move forward with our godly baggage, freely doing what we wish based on
what seems good and best.

Years ago I told my daughter Joy about this freedom. In her mid-twenties
she was trying to figure out God's personal will for her life. At the time, she
was asking God, "Should I stay in L.A. or move to Portland, Oregon?" She
called me for my input and in that conversation I asked her if she had been
doing the four wills. But let's hear her story in her own words.

— A Word from My Daughter Joy —

After I had been working for my dad about four or five months and living in Redondo Beach, California, I was beginning to wonder if La La Land,

where I had lived for the last year, was really the place for me. I had a couple girlfriends up in Portland, Oregon, who I knew would be fun to live near and be the type of people to push me as a person and help me grow in my faith.

I shared with my dad my desire to move, as well as my fear of being someone who was always changing and doing something new. Was I going to be a person who was never content? I also feared not following God's will, because it was something I had always heard Christians say—that many seemed unsure if they were doing it or not. At times they only seemed to mention God's will when they wanted to justify their decision. "Is it God's will that I marry her?" or "I absolutely knew it was God's will I take this job . . ." I desperately wanted a sign from God that told me Portland was where I *had* to live.

Over a hot fudge sundae, I told my dad that I was pretty sure God was giving me those requested signs. Why? *Because* recently I had seen lots of Oregon license plates and T-shirts. Totally God.

That's when my dad (probably trying to conceal his amusement at my license plate from the heavenlies story) graciously told me about the four wills of God.

The conversation essentially went as follows:

> **Dad:** "Here's an idea . . . Why don't you look for T-shirts that say Ohio?
>
> **Me:** [crickets]
>
> **Dad:** Maybe God *is* giving you a sign, but sometimes we can also see what we are looking for and say it's God because that's our desire.
>
> **Me:** [more crickets]
>
> **Dad:** "Joy, have you changed friend groups a lot in high school or college?"
>
> **Me:** "No."
>
> **Dad:** "Did you change colleges or degrees a number of times?"
>
> **Me:** "No."
>
> **Dad:** "So, I don't think we can conclude that you are someone who is a flake or wishy-washy, or will never be content in what you do or who you are loyal to. You may desire something new, but that doesn't mean you are someone who will never be content. What I've seen in Scripture is that there are four key passages that say 'This

is the will of God.' If you are following those, you are free to do as you please and follow those desires—even if that desire is to move to Portland."

Me: "So what are they?"

Dad: "Well, do you believe in Christ as your Savior?"

Me: "Yes."

Dad: "Are you having premarital sex?"

Me: "No."

Dad: "Do you try to give thanks to God?"

Me: "I think so . . ."

Dad: "Are you submissive to authority?"

Me: "Sounds intense but, uhh, I think so?"

Dad: "I am your boss and your father, and your mother and I are telling you that you are free to make this move. If I had reservations about your character or you moving, it would be important for you to listen to that and possibly submit to the reasons for you not going. But you are free. I don't think moving to Portland is an issue of sinning against God's will or not. Make plans to go. And if He doesn't want you there, He will close that door. Have the attitude 'if the Lord wills or permits,' but proceed in freedom."

There was a huge weight lifted off my shoulders. I never forgot that conversation and the delight I felt in seeing that it wasn't as much an issue of God showing me the word *Oregon* emblazoned in the sunset for me to have permission to go; it was the issue of my obedience toward God in some key areas of my life and finding freedom to follow my desires. I was completely free.

Since then, this message helped me as I answered so many questions for young Christians through my work with Love and Respect Now. Many wanted to know if it was God's will that they marry, date, break up with, take this step or that. I was able to encourage them, because of what my dad taught me, that God's will isn't a *Choose Your Own Adventure* novel, where if you choose one page over the other you'll come to find out that, "whoops! you fell into hot lava! THE END!" This was freeing for so many.

=====

I love what Joy shares. Liberty came to her and can come to all of us. In a sense, when we follow these four wills, God allows us the freedom to choose our own adventure.

Of course, in first hearing about this freedom, some get nervous, which I understand and will address throughout the book. This is not a license to sin. Not all choices are good or of God. For instance, as believers in Jesus Christ, we must marry someone who also believes in Jesus Christ (1 Corinthians 7:39). We are not free to marry someone who rejects Jesus Christ. But when all things are equal between two good and acceptable decisions, we can go either way as long as we are following the four wills (and in the case of marriage, so is the other person!). We will not miss God's will when we are doing God's will!

What Sets This Book Apart from Other Teachings on God's Will?

After hearing me teach on the four wills, someone wrote me, "Many think there is a blueprint for a specific will that they have to figure out by prayer and listening or they will horribly miss God's perfect plan. You said 'keep these four wills and do as you please.' That is the answer, and very freeing. But many times, people don't realize that and get frozen in decisions about who to marry, where to go to school, etc., thinking there is only one answer. They wait for God to speak to them through individual signs (i.e., fleeces, small voice, open doors, etc.). I have friends who were taught that model in Christian schools. The four wills really frees them!"

In this book, I explain that we need to pray about life decisions and that God does uniquely lead. He can dramatically reveal to us to take path A, not path B, especially for those in the persecuted church. And, when things seem unclear about His will, this book helps those who fear they will miss God's will and so freeze up, failing to move forward. This book offers biblical criteria to the "frozen" for moving forward or staying put. It also helps those who aggressively but wrongly make decisions based on superficial criteria, like looking for Oregon license plates as a sign or fleece to move to Oregon. In these pages, we will consider the biblical criteria for determining God's will based on God's will! This best enables us to make good and godly decisions over a lifetime. We can move forward or stay put with greater confidence and a clear conscience, even though none of us will make perfect decisions.

Recently we were with friends who heard my quick overview of the four wills, as well as what I reported about my daughter Joy and her experience with the four wills. One man, an intellectual and Harvard graduate and very successful businessman who loves the Lord, said, "When you gave that overview of the four wills, they sounded legalistic to me. But when you told us about Joy's experience, it brought home how freeing this teaching is. Wow. Thank you."

We must never feel bound to a religious and oppressive formula. Utilizing the four wills is not a call to enter a legalistic checklist that enslaves us but an opportunity, as Paul writes, to go about "doing the will of God from the heart" (Ephesians 6:6).

Also, when we are not fully assured which way we should go on a matter, we can meet with a godly, wise person and use the four wills as a checklist to evaluate a decision. When my daughter turned to me, the four wills guided the conversation and provided her with insight and relief.

How about you? Right now, do you have two choices in front of you? You can ask yourself and your friend, "Which decision will most hinder me from following the four wills, and which will most help me follow them? And, because I care to make a difference in my world, which choice will best enable me to help others learn and follow the four wills?" By the way, it isn't enough for a person to ask, "Should I take that job in New York given I follow the four wills?" This individual should also ask, "Should I take my family to New York for this job because that best enables them to follow the four wills?"

Are you ready to dig in? Let's start here!

Chapter 1
DISCOVERING GOD'S WILL

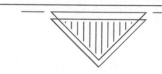

God Has a Will

Since some variation of the words "the will of God" or the "Father's will" occur more than twenty times in the New Testament, it is fair to assume "the will of God" exists and can be known. The apostle Paul commands us to "understand what the will of the Lord is" (Ephesians 5:17). Jesus uses the expression when He addresses God with the words, "Your will be done" in what has come to be known as the Lord's Prayer (Matthew 6:10). Yes, God has a will that we must discover and do from the heart.

Paul declared "the whole purpose of God" (Acts 20:27). There is a body of content between Genesis and Revelation that squarely applies to the church. In less than thirty-six months, Paul taught the Christ-followers this "whole purpose."

We read in Jude 3, "the faith . . . was once for all handed down to the saints." There are boundaries to this content. In fact, Paul warned: "learn not to exceed what is written" (1 Corinthians 4:6).

Epaphras was "always laboring earnestly . . . in his prayers" for the Colossians, that they might "stand perfect and fully assured in all the will of God" (Colossians 4:12). Unfortunately, we can know and do just part of God's will.

How important is it to learn the whole purpose of God and do it from the heart?

Consider Jesus' words in Matthew 7:21: "Not everyone who says to Me, 'Lord, Lord,' will enter the kingdom of heaven, but he who does the will of My Father who is in heaven will enter." Later, He adds, "For whoever does the will of My Father who is in heaven, he is My brother and sister and mother" (Matthew 12:50). John further emphasizes the importance of God's will when he declares, "the one who does the will of God lives forever" (1 John 2:17). Doing the will of God, therefore, not only reveals our relationship to God, but it is also related to our eternal destiny. Concerning eternity, the writer of Hebrews states, "Therefore, do not throw away your confidence, which has a great reward. For you have need of endurance, so that when you have done the will of God, you may receive what was promised" (Hebrews 10:35–36).

From Jesus and the apostles we learn that the will of God never ranks second to anything. For this reason, all of us should be asking, "What is God's will?"

Most of the time when people ask, "What is God's will for my life?" they have in mind a specific concern: career, love relationships, finances, etc. Rarely do people simply ask, "What is God's will, His whole purpose, to which the Bible refers?" The difference between these two questions is crucial to finding God's will for you. I believe that if you start by asking the second question—"What is God's will?"—you will likely discern the answer to the first question, "What is God's will for my life?"

The question, "What is God's will for my life?" considers what I refer to as the unique will of God for me. The question, "What is God's will?" explores what I call the universal will of God for all believers. I contend that the best way to know God's unique will is to know and follow His universal will for all believers, and this book is about four universal wills of God, which serve as a great starting point, as I referenced in the Introduction.

God's Universal Will

The apostle John describes how following the universal leads to the unique. First John 3:21–22 states, "Beloved, if our heart does not condemn us, we have confidence before God; and whatever we ask we receive from Him, because we keep His commandments and do the things that are pleasing in His sight."

There we have it. Keep God's commandments (His universal will in imperative form) and encounter His unique response to our petition. In response, God guides and provides for us at a personal level. We can experience a remarkable answer to prayer, an orchestration of events pointing to a particular course of action, or a supernatural peace in the midst of unanswered prayers. Amazing things can happen as we keep His universal commandments and then ask Him to uniquely direct our steps.

God's Four Universal Wills

Though all of God's commands in the Old and New Testament that apply to the church fall under God's will for us, God reveals in four passages, four specific wills. I refer to them as the four wills of God.

Like on a map, it is as though God declares, "Start Here!"

This doesn't mean we can ignore the rest of God's commands, only that we probably will ignore the rest if we ignore these four.

These four wills, or commands, are found in four passages that identify precisely the will of God. These four specifically declare "this is" or "such is" the will of God. These passages are matchless. No other verses identify God's will with such exactness.

What are these four?

> John 6:40: "**This is the will of my Father** that everyone who beholds the Son and believes in Him will have eternal life and I Myself will raise him up on the last day" (emphasis added).

> 1 Thessalonians 5:18: "In everything give thanks; **for this is God's will for you** in Christ Jesus" (emphasis added).

1 Peter 2:13–15: "Submit yourselves for the Lord's sake to every human institution, whether to a king as the one in authority, or to governors as sent by him for the punishment of evildoers and the praise of those who do right. **For such is the will of God** that by doing right you may silence the ignorance of foolish men" (emphasis added).

1 Thessalonians 4:3: "**For this is the will of God,** your sanctification; that is, that you abstain from sexual immorality" (emphasis added).

In other words:

Believe in Jesus Christ.
Give thanks in everything.
Submit in doing right.
Abstain from sexual sin.

These four wills are divinely highlighted in gold, so to speak. God intends for these four to stand out. Follow these and you are in the best position to have confidence He will reveal His unique will to you as you ask Him to lead you, as the apostle John taught.

God's Unique Will

All of us long for God to uniquely lead and bless our lives. But is that a valid desire? Does God have a unique will for us?

Scripture tells us God designed us and knew us before we were born: He "knit [us] together in [our] mother's womb" (Psalm 139:13 NIV). Even when we feel totally lost, God knows everything about us and our circumstances. As the psalmist says, "I will counsel you with My eye upon you" (Psalm 32:8). Though we may pursue or plan many things, "the LORD will continually guide you" (Isaiah 58:11) because your steps are directed or "ordained" by Him (Psalm 37:23; Proverbs 20:24).

We believe such Scriptures as these: "He will make your paths straight" (Proverbs 3:5–6), ". . . your plans will be established" (Proverbs 16:3), "the

LORD directs his steps" (Proverbs 16:9), and "if any of you lacks wisdom . . . it will be given to him" (James 1:5).

God responds to our good and personal desires. Psalm 20:4 says, "May He grant you your heart's desire and fulfill all your counsel!" Psalm 21:2 states, "You have given him his heart's desire, and You have not withheld the request of his lips." We read in Psalm 145:19, "He will fulfill the desire of those who fear Him; He will also hear their cry and will save them."

We would be hard-pressed to argue that God is not interested in being personally involved in the believer's life!

As the apostle John told us in 1 John 3:21–22, when we keep His commandments and do what is pleasing in His sight, then whatever we ask—as individuals in specific circumstances—we receive from Him.

Listen to three amazing stories of God actively involved in the personal lives of believers.

Sam!

Let me illustrate with a godly father and mother of a daughter that I learned about from my friend Paul Lewis. This husband and wife walked with God, trusting and obeying Him faithfully. Here's what happened.

One summer this family of three from southern California went hiking in Oregon. As they trekked in the woods, they found a Bible lying on a huge rock. Because the Bible evidenced no weather damage, they concluded the owner had recently left it there. Though the cover had the name "Sam" on it, there was no further identification. As the father thumbed through the pages, he noticed heavy underlining, exclamation points, and devotional comments that indicated that Sam possessed a vibrant relationship with Jesus. Not knowing what to do with the Bible, the family took it home with them.

One day the parents were interceding for their daughter and felt led to pray for a future spouse. The spiritual passion of Sam came to mind, and they found this prayer surging from their hearts: "God, please send a man to marry our daughter who loves you as much as Sam, that young man." Since Sam's faith so clearly reflected their hopes for their daughter, they simplified the prayer over the years to "Send us a Sam!"

What parents would not smile when four years later they learned that their daughter, now in college, was dating a guy named Sam? One weekend this Sam offered to help the family move across town. While carting boxes from the house to the moving trailer, he saw a book slide out. When Sam picked it up, he was stunned to realize that he was holding his long-lost Bible. "Where did you get that Bible?" he asked in amazement. "That's my Bible!"

Indeed, that was Sam's Bible. Not only did God send a Sam, He sent *the* Sam! And, Sam eventually married their daughter.

Such a story should send chills up our spine!

We can receive from God what we ask from Him. We can experience the unique moving of God for our lives. He knows us by name in a very intimate way (Philippians 4:3; Revelation 21:27) and responds as though we alone exist!

$1,500!

For Marilyn, a friend of mine from Holland, Michigan, God demonstrated His unique and wonderful will. Marilyn recounts an incident in which she and her husband found themselves $1,500 short of what they thought they had in their bank account. When they figured out that Marilyn's husband had mistakenly recorded one $1,500 deposit twice, he said, "Marilyn, don't write any more checks. I've really made a mess, and we are $1,500 overdrawn." Then they prayed together and asked for God's help.

That night they went to their weekly church supper that cost $10.50 for the family to eat. Marilyn asked the Lord how to pay for this since they were overdrawn and could not pay for the meal with a check. She then remembered she had fifty cents in her purse and ten dollars she was saving to put toward her husband's Christmas present. Though she didn't want to use the gift money, she thanked God for reminding her of it. However, that night when she came to the counter to pay for their meals, the woman said, "Someone already paid for your dinner tonight."

Marilyn told me, "For eighteen years I had eaten at this church potluck and no one—not one—had ever paid for our family until this night!" Clearly, God understood her unique plight, small as it might seem, and responded. Emboldened by this divine moment, Marilyn asked God to supply the $1,500. After she told her husband about her prayer of faith, he called every day and jokingly asked, "Well, did you get a check through the mail?" Together they would laugh, though she kept praying.

Ten days later a big envelope arrived that was marked "Express Mail." Since her husband usually received "that kind of mail," she left it on the counter. When she later recognized the names of good friends on the envelope, she decided to open it. Inside she found two small envelopes. When she opened the first one, she found a check for $1,500! In utter amazement, she opened the second envelope and found a note saying, "Accept this gift, not from us but from the Lord." When her husband came home that night and learned of the check, he was so awed that he called the family together to thank the Lord for His specific answer to their prayer.

When Marilyn decided to call these friends that very night to thank them, she was eager to learn why they gave that amount. She inquired, "Why did you send $1,500, why not $10 or $100 or even $200?" Her friend replied, "Well, we had both been impressed in our prayer time together that you had a financial need, but we didn't know how much. We decided to separate for a time to pray on our own, asking God to reveal to us how much we should give. When we came back together, the Lord had impressed upon both of us the amount of $1,500."

Wow! Is your heart leaping at the possibilities of God answering your prayers? Do you desire God to reveal His unique will to you in ways that mirror these examples?

France

What I can say is that when we fully surrender our hearts to God's will for our lives without fear and with holy anticipation, good things begin to happen. Some people who attended my church shared their experience with me. The day Steve and Brenda Nesbitt fully surrendered their lives to serve Christ in France, they went to a local supermarket near their home in Royal Oak, Michigan. In this time of surrender to God's call to serve overseas, they prayed, "Lord, we will go to Ronchin," which is a little town outside of Lille, France. After that prayer time, just one hour later, they needed to pick some things up at the store. While they were shopping, they overheard someone speaking French, so they engaged this person in conversation, and in passing said they were headed to France. The man asked where and they said, "Lille." The man replied, "That is where I am from!" Then Steve said, "Well actually it is a little town just outside of that." When he named the town of Ronchin, the man said, "That is exactly where I am from!"

Afterward, Steve and Brenda asked the question, "What are the odds of surrendering our lives to Jesus Christ completely and God confirming that surrender a few moments later by having some French person from the very village you are going to meet you in a store in Royal Oak?" This was no coincidence to them.

Almost three years after moving to France, something else happened. After looking at great length for a house to rent in Ronchin, the Nesbitts finally found one that was suitable. The owner was unavailable to give them the key on the day they were to move in, but said the elderly couple who lived next door had a copy of the key. When they arrived at the neighbors' place to get the key, the neighbor lady learned that Steve and Brenda were Americans from the Detroit area in the U.S. and commented, "Well, that is interesting, I have a son in Royal Oak, Michigan. You wouldn't by any chance have ever met him?" And of course they had. (And that elderly couple became like adoptive grandparents to the Nesbitt children.)

So, how can we encounter these kinds of answers to prayer? I believe when we start with the four universal wills of God we position ourselves in the best way to trigger God's moving in our lives. This book is about the triggering effect!

The Trigger

When a person lives to do the will of God, such obedience is what triggers a distinct encounter with the living God. These encounters are personal, and have no exact replication anywhere else in the world. Yes, others will experience similar leadings but just as each unique individual's name is written in the Book of Life (Revelation 3:5), each individual's leading and life story is precious and unique too.

When I say our obedience "triggers" God's active response in our lives, I do not mean some kind of mechanical process that handcuffs God. Such an idea would be irreverent. He is not bound to us. He has no obligation to do our bidding. This is not like a series of dominos that fall in line because we have coerced God into intervening. This is not a hocus-pocus approach to God Almighty.

A better image might be that our obedience touches the heart of God who loves us and desires to show us favor and blessing. Said another way, "God things" do not happen when we refuse to follow God's will. The psalmist exclaimed, "If I regard wickedness in my heart, the Lord will not hear" (Psalm 66:18). Most of us know that God will not respond in the way we are describing when we do not fulfill the conditions that warm His heart toward us.

Will God respond every day, all day? No, not visibly to us or according to what we dream about. Though we long for God's personal and powerful moving in our lives with signs, wonders, and miracles on a daily basis, that won't happen. It didn't happen with the apostles or the prophets. Many years passed, even decades, between the dramatic stories we read about in the Bible. Even with our Lord, there is nothing miraculous mentioned after His birth except at age twelve when He astounded the Jewish leaders in the temple with His knowledge. From age twelve to thirty we have no record of anything supernatural happening. Then at the beginning of His ministry, at around age thirty, He turned the water into wine at the wedding at Cana.

Thus, I will not over-promise here about your experience of supernatural encounters. The Son of God lived eighteen years without any testimony that miracles transpired in His life. However, when we trust and obey Him, there will be moments here and there throughout our lives when He manifests Himself in ways that send chills up our spines with awe over His kindnesses. This happens because we have chosen to follow His will.

Though all of us must continue to grapple with "the whole purpose of God" (Acts 20:27), we must take our first step somewhere. This book urges us to start with the four wills. This places us in the best position to ask with confidence for God to uniquely listen and lead.

Let me add. Sarah, my wife, and I start again and again with these four wills as various issues and decisions arise. We have known these four wills for nearly four decades so this book isn't just for a new believer but one who has followed Christ for years, and that's why this is so exciting, rich, and meaningful. "Start Here" means "Start Here Again." Sarah and I find real joy and confidence in moving forward in life since even if we do not receive what we ask, we know we are in the center of God's will as we actively believe in Jesus Christ, abstain from sexual sin, give thanks in everything, and submit in doing right, and help others believe, abstain, give thanks, and submit (B.A.G.S.). At the end of the day, we know that as we trust and obey these four wills we please God, and in pleasing Him we find pleasure. We are content either way! As with you, we want to imitate Christ. Jesus said, "For I have come down from heaven, not to do My own will, but the will of Him who sent Me" (John 6:38).

But let's consider a few questions in the next chapter that all of us need to answer for ourselves.

Do we really want to do His will?

Chapter 2
IMPORTANT QUESTIONS

What Is Your Motive?

When it comes to seeking the will of God, I suspect some of us are a little bit like Johnny. His seventh birthday was coming, and he knew exactly what he wanted for his birthday present: a brand-new bike. For weeks, he pestered his mom with the words, "I want a bike. You need to get me a bike!" But because he had been disobedient in recent days, his mom used his demanding attitude as a teaching moment.

"Johnny," she says, "I can't believe you are demanding a bike. You have not been on your best behavior over the last several weeks. I think you need to think about your conduct. I want you to go to the bedroom for a 'time-out' and think about how you have been acting. In fact, I want you to write a letter to God telling Him why you should get a bike, and then let's talk about this."

Begrudgingly, Johnny goes upstairs to his bedroom, sits down at his desk, takes some paper and a pencil and begins to write: "Dear God, this is Johnny. I've been really good. Give me a bike." He soon sees his untruthfulness about being really good. He tears up the letter and starts again: "Dear God, this is Johnny. I've been pretty good. Give me a bike."

But, he knows deep down that he has not even been pretty good. So, he tears up his letter and begins again: "Dear God, this is Johnny. I've been really bad. Give me a bike." He instantly sees that God won't buy this argument either since God won't reward bad behavior even if the truthful confession might get mercy. So, he tears up this letter too.

Suddenly, he gets an idea. He jumps up from his chair and runs downstairs through the kitchen. As he passes his mother, he tells her he is going to the church on the corner. She thinks, *Wow, he's getting serious about this prayer thing.* She is elated.

Johnny runs down the street and up the sidewalk to the Catholic Church. He enters the front door leading to the sanctuary, hurries down the aisle, goes up on the altar, and grabs an eighteen-inch statue of Mary. When he returns, he goes in the back door of the house so his mom can't see him. He heads upstairs to his bedroom to resume writing his letter to God.

Placing the statue of Mary on his desk in front of him, he pens, "Dear God, this is Johnny. Give me a bike! I've got Your mother!" Are you laughing?

Even at seven we try to come up with ways to manipulate God to fulfill our desires. I don't know if this story really happened, but I laugh at how it reflects that truth of our nature!

Sometimes we approach God with a selfish agenda. Our prayers are all about us and our desires. It is all about our will, not God's will. In effect, we are saying, "God, give me what I want. I've got Your mother."

Guess what? Our all-wise and all-just God will not answer such prayers.

Today, as well as in the first century, some folks try to get God to give them what they crave. James writes, "You ask and do not receive, because you ask with wrong motives so that you may spend it on your pleasures" (James 4:3). When we approach God with wrong motives, we are trying to manipulate God.

In contending that we can do as we please as we follow the four wills, we are not referring to the kind of pleasure that James addresses. The Greek word James uses is *hedonais* from which we get hedonistic. All of us must recognize the self-indulgent and unrestrained pleasure-seeking to which James directs our attention.

Having said this, I doubt that many of us reading this book are asking God to enable us to live a hedonistic lifestyle. That's not our prayer. Our problem is that we think our motives are good when praying but fail to discern that we are seeking more of our own will than God's will, and we do not detect this.

Is This about Your Will or God's Will?

In the church where I served as a pastor, there was a sacred occasion called "child dedication." The ceremony gives parents an opportunity to publicly commit their children to the Lord as Samuel's mother, Hannah, and Mary and Joseph did (1 Samuel 1:28; Luke 2:22). As I met privately with the parents of one child being dedicated, something prompted me to ask, "Why are you dedicating your child to the Lord?" They replied that they were doing this so that God would protect their child from bad things. Their comment piqued my curiosity, so I asked, "Let me see if I understand you. Are you doing this because you believe that after you dedicate your child to God, God is obligated to protect your child from all evil?" Surprisingly, they answered "yes" to that question.

"Well, actually it doesn't work this way," I explained. "To be more accurate, this is a *parent* dedication. You are dedicating yourself to bring your child up in the ways of Jesus Christ whether or not your child responds. Truth be told, you can only control your parenting; you cannot control the ultimate outcomes in your children. So, we are calling you to parent God's way even if your child chooses to reject Jesus Christ.

"God the Father," I continued, "models for us what we as parents must include in our worldview: the reality of evil. The Bible reveals that suffering and evil can come to Christ's followers. As parents we need to instruct our children as best we can to understand the reality of suffering and evil and how to deal with it as God intends. Yes, we should ask God to protect our children, but that prayer does not guarantee protection against all evil. This is not some kind of insurance policy."

What the parents said next surprised me: "If God is not going to protect our child, we are not going to do this."

What is going on here with these parents?

They are reversing the purpose of the dedication ceremony. Their obedience to God is conditional on God's fulfillment of their wishes. They do not want to do God's will, by being the parents God calls them to be, but want

God to do their will which entails keeping their child from drugs and other temptations, or from anything that would embarrass them socially. In effect, they are praying, "Not *Your* will, but *my* will be done."

These parents did not perceive the extent of their manipulation because they cared about their child and were looking to God, so how could they be wrong? But God is holy and just, not some Santa Claus figure here to do our bidding. God will not be manipulated just because we care about our kids and are praying for their safety. As James wrote: ". . . you ask with wrong motives" (James 4:3).

Getting in tune with motive is foremost to James. When we do not, down the road we will be disillusioned and resentful when God fails to do what we asked because we will convince ourselves we care more than God cares. If these parents had dedicated their child to God according to their thinking, what would they feel when this child, now a teenager, made sinful choices during a stretch that left these parents in heart-wrenching pain? Would these parents blame God for failing to uphold His end of the bargain?

Sadly, we observe some people walking away from the faith for precisely this reason. There comes a moment when what they expected God to do, God did not do, and then they blame God rather than discern their impure motive and unbiblical thinking. They conclude that God lacks the love and power that they thought He possessed for their purposes. They end up resenting and rejecting Him because their theology had no place for a cross.

This does not mean, as I mentioned, that we hold back from praying for God's protection of our children. We must pray for God's protection. James says we have not because we ask not (James 4:2). We must ask. But when we do pray, we pray with the mind-set that concludes the prayer with, "Not my will but Your will be done." Our inner posture according to James 4:15 is to be, "If the Lord wills." We believe God sees the bigger picture.

We must remind ourselves that we live in a fallen world. People sin against us. We sin. Our children sin. Because sin entered the world, physical death awaits us. No amount of petition will change this biblical teaching (Romans 5:12). Even after God raised Lazarus from the dead, eventually Lazarus died again. God will not protect us from ultimately dying.

So, when it comes to praying for the protection of our children, each of us must be honest with ourselves, and discern why we are praying. Is this from a heart that says, "God, You have an absolute obligation to keep my child from evil"? If so, this is dictatorial praying, not meek praying. One must never say that God has an absolute obligation to protect our children from temptations and pain. Instead, we need to instruct our children that there is temptation and pain in the world, and live before them in such a way that we show them how to endure difficulties and resist carnal attractions. This is parent dedication, and we can rightly pray this for ourselves.

Why do some good-willed people miss this biblical perspective? They select certain promises in the Bible and ignore the other portions of Scripture that make them feel uncomfortable.

Can a Person Fixate on Select Promises in the Bible While Ignoring Other Portions?

A woman prayed for the birth of her daughter's first child. Soon after the delivery, the precious baby died. This minutes-long grandmother not only shared her pain but her disillusionment with God's promises. She kept Bible verses in a promise box and prayed over these promises for protection, health, and joy related to the soon-to-be baby. This is a good thing except when she encountered the opposite. She then shut down on God. Later she confessed that she only searched for beneficial promises in Scripture, skipping over any verses pertaining to the unexplained suffering of the righteous. She humbly acknowledged that she ignored the many portions of the Bible that tell us that bad things happen to godly people, including the loss of loved ones, and that not all of God's promises are experienced by all of God's people.

We read in Hebrews 11:35–39, "others were tortured . . . others experienced mockings and scourgings, yes, also chains and imprisonment. They were stoned, they were sawn in two, they were tempted, they were put to death with the sword; they went about in sheepskins, in goatskins, being destitute, afflicted, ill-treated . . . wandering in deserts and mountains and caves and holes in the ground. And all these, having gained approval through their faith, did not receive what was promised."

Note the last phrase, "did not receive what was promised." They did not receive the earthly promises that many of us fixate on in the Scriptures. This did not mean God was unfaithful and unkind, but that God's will may include unexplained suffering. Even Jesus on the cross asked why. "My God,

My God, why have You forsaken Me?" (Matthew 27:46). There are things we will not understand about suffering and unfulfilled promises. But we can know we are pleasing God—gaining approval through our faith—as we apply the four wills and help others apply them.

While in Los Angeles, I spoke at the First Chinese Baptist Church. I met a woman who told me of her grandfather who lived for Christ in China. When persecution flooded the country, he had his wife and daughter escape to America while he and their two sons would remain. Because China closed off to the rest of the world, they never learned the fate of the father and sons until President Nixon reopened travel to and from China. This woman, who was the daughter of that daughter, then found out the story of her grandfather and two uncles. The grandfather had been educated outside of China so was viewed as an intellectual with foreign leanings and known to be a Christian. At that time, these were two horrible characteristics for a Chinese citizen. Because of this, he and his two sons were brought before the authorities. He was told to renounce his faith in Jesus Christ or one of the sons would be shot right there in front of him. He refused and they shot and killed his son. They let the other boy go. The dad was forced for the rest of his life to sweep streets and wear a sign that said, "Foreign educated."

The unique will of God is governed by the universal will of God. Believing in Jesus Christ can trigger persecution, pain, and death. Such a man reflects what we read about in Hebrews 11.

How sad when people do not pay close attention to significant portions of Scripture that do not fit the narrative they prefer.

Sarah and I retain a vivid memory from the early 1970s of my aunt (now deceased) adversely judging me. I wanted my aunt to meet Sarah so we went to her home for a social visit. I had recently come to Christ and shared with my aunt, who was a schoolteacher, that I planned to enter the ministry. As I spoke of my intentions, my aunt's countenance changed. A look of disgust appeared on her face as I talked. It was so distracting I stopped and asked what I had said that troubled her. Then with hostility—which I had never seen in her or from her—she denounced my decision to go into the ministry. Dumbfounded by her out-of-character deportment, I asked, "Why are you so angry over this?"

Steaming, she replied, "You are wasting your mind. You should be a lawyer."

I replied, "I don't want to be a lawyer." As I sat there for a few seconds, I became vividly aware that her reaction was unrelated to me going into the ministry so I asked, "What's this anger all about?"

She astonished Sarah and me when she blurted out, "When I was a little girl I prayed for a bicycle. The minister told us if we asked and really believed, then God would give us what we asked. I prayed and prayed and prayed but I never got a bike! I decided then and there that I would not believe in God."

Despite this being one of the most childish comments I've ever heard from an adult, I empathize in part with her disappointment. Every child must grapple with faith, just as every adult must grapple with asking of God. Each person must try to make sense out of what the Bible tells us about asking and receiving from God. Many have read the words of Jesus, "Ask, and it will be given to you; seek, and you will find; knock, and it will be opened to you. For everyone who asks receives, and he who seeks finds, and to him who knocks it will be opened" (Matthew 7:7–8).

Did Jesus in His Incarnation Always Receive What He Asked?

Part of the answer is that we must look at other portions of Scripture that shed light on how to interpret the Scriptures that tell us that we can ask and will receive. In this case, my aunt should have kept reading her Bible. Every text of Scripture has a larger context. As Bible teachers say, "If you don't know how to interpret a passage, keep reading." For example, my aunt should have looked at the story of Jesus in the garden of Gethsemane. There we see Him asking something of the Father but not receiving—and if anyone had perfect faith Jesus did! Unfortunately, my aunt shut down and quit reading. She let one negative experience determine her loss of faith for a lifetime. And, had she read James who exhorted us to pray from pure motives, perhaps she would have changed the nature of her prayer from "Give me a bike" to "Provide me with a bike to give to an orphan."

As for Jesus praying and not receiving, it is stunning. Jesus was perfect, and the perfect Son of God prayed three times and did not receive what He requested. We read in Matthew 26:44 that He "prayed a third time." Theologians refer to it as "thrice praying." What did He pray? We read in

Luke 22:42 that Jesus asked, "Father, if You are willing, remove this cup from Me." He asked three times that He could take an avenue other than going to the cross in a torturous crucifixion. In His humanity, He recognized the immeasurable pain that awaited Him. However, the heavenly Father did not respond to this specific request because of the bigger picture. Because of this we hear Jesus pray, "yet not My will, but Yours be done." The will of the Father for Jesus countermanded what Jesus personally asked in His humanity during His incarnation.

We observe Paul praying three times in 2 Corinthians 12:7–9. "There was given me a thorn in the flesh, a messenger of Satan to torment me—to keep me from exalting myself! Concerning this I implored the Lord three times that it might leave me. And He has said to me, 'My grace is sufficient for you, for power is perfected in weakness.'" The unique will of God for Paul countermanded what Paul asked to be the unique will of the Father for him!

Though you are not going to the cross like Jesus, nor given the same thorn in the flesh as Paul, even so, you can walk in obedience to the four wills of God, ask in prayer and not receive. That does not mean you are failing to keep His commandments and do the things that are pleasing in His sight, which John addresses in 1 John 3:21–22. Nor does it mean that God is some kind of cosmic killjoy out to ruin your life by telling you to trust Him and then pulling the rug out from under your feet. What it means is that your heavenly Father sees the bigger picture and acts according to His omniscience.

Only the skeptic and mocker calls this a cop-out. They like to argue that prayer is pointless and what will happen will happen. They argue that Christians are trying to soothe themselves with the false idea that the bad things that come their way are really part of God's greater good. But for them, any thinking person spurns this fairy-tale mind-set. As Karl Marx famously declared, "Religion is the opium of the people." Each of us must make a decision about our worldview. Everyone will believe something based on something or someone. What will we believe? I prefer the view of Jesus! Jesus tells us Abba Father is there, He cares, and He calls us to pray and trust Him. The beloved of Jesus, the apostle John, writes in 1 John 5:14–15: "This is the confidence which we have before Him, that, if we ask anything according to His will, He hears us. And if we know that He hears us in whatever we ask, we know that we have the requests which we have asked from Him."

I have chosen to trust this worldview. To John, we can have confidence that God is very real and present and listening.

Will God always grant our request? To John, the caveat is that we must ask "according to His will." Again, God sees the bigger picture, and Father knows best! As most of us have heard: He is God and we are not. However, His lack of response is not because we lack faith or because He does not care. He cares and we have faith but in this instance it is not in accordance with His will and His kingdom purposes. We must walk by faith, not sight (2 Corinthians 5:7).

For certain we must not mock prayer as pointless. The prophets of old prayed. The apostles in the first century prayed. Our Lord prayed, commanded us to pray, and assumed we would pray (Matthew 6:9; Luke 11:1–2). Thus, when God seems silent in response to our petitions, we must trust in His supervision; His "super" vision.

Is There a Silver Lining in Not Receiving an Answer to Prayer?

On a different note, in our daily living and decision-making, His silence can mean we are free to do what seems good and best. Many times we face a fork in the road and we pray, "Dear Lord, please show me which path to take." But there is no clear leading. This could very well mean that God gives us the freedom to choose our own course. Not to be trite but something akin to those children's novels that allow us to choose our own adventure.

God delights in giving us an incredible scope of thought and action. For instance, even at the beginning of creation we read in Genesis 2:19, "Out of the ground the Lord God formed every beast of the field and every bird of the sky, and brought them to the man to see what he would call them; and whatever the man called a living creature, that was its name."

How wonderful that toward Adam God not only gave the freedom to name the animals but God seems joyfully curious "to see what he would call them."

A simplistic analogy would be that of endurance racing for motor vehicles. They begin at point A and travel to point B, sometimes for 1,000 miles, like the Baja 1000. During the course, they have a great deal of flexibility

within the boundaries of the rules and track. Given our life is like an endurance race, we have a great deal of freedom within the confines of the world
in which we live, move, and breathe. Though God has firmly established and
predestined certain boundaries on our planet, we have thousands of good
choices. We can steer this way or that based on our interests, abilities, and
opportunities.

As for preferences, God has designed His world and kingdom in such a
way that He allows us to make decisions based on personal opinions (Romans
14:1), personal judgments (14:2), personal persuasions (14:14), personal
convictions (14:22), personal happiness (14:22), and personal faith (14:23).
There are gray areas that the apostle Paul addressed in Romans 14 that allow
a great deal of latitude among believers. Within much of our daily living—
the race we are running—we have the freedom to direct our own steps, as the
subtitle of this book states.

The same applies to spiritual gifting. God provides each believer with
at least one spiritual gift among the nineteen spiritual gifts mentioned in
1 Corinthians 12, Romans 12, Ephesians 4, and 1 Peter 4. Paul states in
1 Corinthians 12:11 that God distributes "to each one individually just as He
wills." What is mathematically amazing is that Paul states, "there are varieties
of gifts . . . and there are varieties of ministries . . . [and] there are varieties of
effects" (12:4–6). The opportunities before an individual are nearly endless.
A person with the gift of teaching (one of the nineteen) can teach in ministries to adults or to children, and the effect among adults can be that one
teaches on marriage or one teaches on finances. With children, one can teach
about God's love or teach about how to get along with people. The effects
are limitless. Nineteen spiritual gifts can be used in any one ministry among
all those happening around the world and within each of those ministries
one has nearly an endless number of possible effects. It turns exponential. All
that to say, God provides mind-boggling freedom to each gifted individual to
decide the ministry and effect.

Back to my daughter Joy. She could turn right or left. She was free to
stay in L.A. or move to Portland, Oregon. As long as she practiced the four
wills, she was free to go or stay based on her desires, gifting, and convictions.
I conveyed to her that she would not hear an angel from heaven announce,
"Thus, saith the Lord! Joy move to Portland, east side of the city, facing north

from apartment A1 on the corner of River Street and Main." Instead, she was free to do as she wished, to do what seemed good and best.

Because moving to Portland or staying in L.A. was not a choice between good and evil, though bad stuff happens in both cities, she could do ministry with fruitful effectiveness for me in either place. She could relax as long as she acted on the four wills. Perhaps we could liken it to a test with ten multiple choices of good things about L.A. and ten about Portland. Joy had the freedom to take her pick and tally her score and go to the place she wished.

"But Emerson, is it really biblical to say a person is free to do as they wish?"

The Freedom of Choice with Regard to Marriage

Why am I so bold in making the point that Joy was free to do as she wished? I observed a revolutionary principle in the New Testament. This was not about moving or not moving but about personal freedom to do as one wishes. One such example pertained to remarriage. In 1 Corinthians 7:39 Paul addresses widows who wondered about their present condition. Paul declares, "A wife is bound as long as her husband lives; but if her husband is dead, she is free to be married to whom she wishes, only in the Lord."

People who contend that women in the first century had little say need to meditate on this text of the holy Word. This widow was free to marry anyone she wished in the Lord. It was her call. She could marry Joseph the Jew in the Lord or she could marry Nicholas the Greek in the Lord. Or, she could remain unmarried, like Paul. She had any number of choices on her multiple-choice test, none of which were intrinsically wrong. She could choose her own adventure based on her personal wishes. However, she could not choose to be married and remain unmarried at the same time, nor could she marry both men at the same time. There are boundaries on our race track. And in this instance, marrying a Christ-follower—in the Lord—was a boundary. Often we observe conditions that God places on various behaviors.

Paul did not apply this freedom teaching solely to the widow. The widow served as one example of where the teaching on personal freedom kicked in. In fact, this idea of freedom was so revolutionary, as Jews came out from under an oppressive legalism, that some people needed to be reminded that this unprecedented freedom still had boundaries. In his writings, he urges Christ-followers never to take advantage of this God-given freedom to direct one's own steps.

The Freedom of Choice Must Be Self-Monitored

Consider these verses:

> Galatians 5:13: "For you were called to freedom, brethren; only *do* not *turn* your freedom into an opportunity for the flesh."

> 1 Corinthians 8:9: "But take care that this liberty of yours does not somehow become a stumbling block to the weak."

> 1 Peter 2:16: "*Act* as free men, and do not use your freedom as a covering for evil, but *use it* as bondslaves of God."

Paul cautions believers against directing their own steps into sinful territory for hedonistic purposes. Don't crash through the guardrails on the race track.

The four wills serve as a guide and governor that prevent us from abusing our freedom. As long as we continue to believe in Jesus Christ and make Him central to our heart and mind, abstain from sexual sin in a culture that continually entices us to cross the line, give thanks to God in the tough times, and submit in doing what is right when doing wrong better advances our self-serving interests, we will not turn our freedom into an opportunity to do carnal things.

It is here I need to address honesty. We can enjoy the freedom God offers, but we must be honest with ourselves about the lines that must never be crossed. It is easy to rationalize, which I define as rational lies. For instance, if we know that we have a problem with alcoholism, then the boundary for us is to avoid those settings that ignite this appetite. What makes this tough is that we may have a friend who has no problem with alcohol, so he can enter a restaurant that serves intoxicating beverages without a second thought. His freedom on his race track is not our freedom. We need to be gut honest about this, and stay in the lane our conscience clearly tells us to stay in. In this instance, we must submit in doing what is right for us, according to one of the four wills. Thus, when our friend invites us to dine with him at the new brewery, we need to propose a creative alternative that respects the friendship but guards our godly heart. We are not free to do what enslaves us.

We Have Freedom to Choose but It Must Be Based on What Seems Good

When the decision before us seems good and brings no harm, based on the available information before us, we can make the decision in good faith. We are free to direct our steps.

By way of analogy, as physicians practice medicine, they must make subjective decisions at life-and-death moments. When they do, many abide by the Hippocratic Oath. Historically, it comes from the Epidemics, which are part of the works of the Greek physician Hippocrates. We read, "The physician must . . . have two special objects in view with regard to disease, namely, to do good or to do no harm."[1]

Does this mean the doctor will automatically save the patient's life? The patient may still die. However, when the physician's choices are reviewed and the supervising body asks, "Did you seek to do good and do no harm?" the doctor can say with a clear conscience, "Yes." Based on the most complete information available, it was the best decision the doctor could make. Though a year later a drug came on the market that could have saved the patient, that drug was not known or obtainable at the time.

Is It Biblical to Say One Can Do What Seems Good and Best?

One of the most significant events in the history of the church needs to be mentioned. We read about it in Acts 15. The apostles had to make a major decision for the whole church throughout all ages. How did they make the decision? They did what "seemed good" (Acts 15:28). In fact, four times in this chapter (Acts 15:22, 25, 28, 34), Luke tells us they did what "seemed good."

The reason this expression of "seemed good" is so important is that two chapters earlier God spoke miraculously about His will. We read in Acts 13:2, "While they were ministering to the Lord and fasting, the Holy Spirit said, 'Set apart for Me Barnabas and Saul for the work to which I have called them.'" I am unsure all that this means but they testified that "the Holy Spirit said." In other words, this was miraculous and unequivocal. But we then come to chapter 15 where the church leaders struggle with whether or not to circumcise Gentiles who had come to Christ. One would think God would clearly speak His will to them on this doctrinal matter that outweighed two missionaries being called to a work. But He didn't, and this matter had the potential of splitting the church down the middle between Jew and Gentile.

As you recall, the first believers were Jews who came to Christ. They were already circumcised. Naturally, when the Gentiles came to Christ, the Jews would conclude that the Gentiles needed to undergo circumcision. What should the early church leaders decide on this critical matter? There is no heavenly voice saying, "Do not have the Gentiles circumcised." Instead, God expected the leaders to use their human judgment (Acts 15:19) in their discussion about this issue and decide based on what "seemed good."

This process of doing what seems good applies to us. For example, we must address and manage a life-and-death situation with our grandfather. Should we keep Grandfather on life support or take him off life support? We pray and pray for an answer. However, there seems to be no clear direction from the Lord and a decision must be made. What should we do? We can proceed with the understanding that God intends for us to deliberate and discuss the issues with other godly and/or wise people. God expects us to exercise our discernment and make a decision.

After we have weighed the factors, if the option we favor seems good, and others agree that it is not an inherently bad selection, we are free to proceed with that course of action. We need not live in fear that we made a devilish decision. At the moment we resolved to go a certain direction, we did so based on the best information we possessed. Though that choice may end up to be a bad decision, we need not second-guess ourselves given we did what "seemed good" at the time.

If after we take Grandfather off life support and he dies, then a new drug comes to the market that might have helped Grandfather and possibly brought him out of the coma, should we enter shame and guilt and plead with God to forgive us? No. At the time, we did not know about the breakthrough drug. We had no such information. We must not conclude, "We made a bad decision." It was not a deplorable plan but an appropriate weighing of the pros and cons based on the facts we had at the time. When we do what seems good and best, we can live with a clear conscience. We are free to live this way. Even if after Grandfather dies no new information arises about life-saving drugs, in doing what seemed good, we acknowledge the decision is subjective. It seemed good. Many times in life we must adhere to this language, "It appeared good to us . . . we had the impression this was a good course . . . this choice struck us as a good decision."[2]

Some Choices Are Better Than Others

"But Emerson, back to this widow in 1 Corinthians 7 who was free to marry whomever in the Lord. Might Joseph be a better man than Nicholas?"

Yes. For this reason we need to be thoughtful about choosing the best among the good choices. Many times we must decide which is better and best for ourselves. In saying that we are free to go this way or that on the race track, I am not arguing that the choice between two good things is always equal. It rarely is six of one and half a dozen of another, and actually this helps tip the scale toward one way or another. Often it could be a 7 to 5 ratio, in favor of the choice with the best merit for us at this season. In Joy's case, Portland scored 7 and L.A. 5 because many of her best Christian friends were moving there and the pull of that wholesome friendship and godly fellowship tipped the scale toward Oregon. In the case of the widow, she might have chosen Joseph because he wanted three children, the number she envisioned, whereas Nicholas only wanted one child. It is wise to look at the pros and cons and weigh them, doing what seems best for us.

Let me add, taking Grandfather off life support or keeping him on life support is a decision between two things that don't seem good. We do not want him to die and we do not want him to suffer by keeping him alive without a quality of life. Neither is a good thing to us, but we must still proceed by deciding what is best between the two choices under the circumstances.

Freedom to Do What Seems Best Is a Biblical Idea

I love the biblical language of discerning and deciding about what is best between two choices as captured in these texts in the New International Version:

> 2 Corinthians 8:10: "And here is my judgment about what is best for you in this matter."

> Philippians 1:10: "That you may be able to discern what is best . . ."

> 1 Thessalonians 3:1: "We thought it best . . ."

If we don't know which to select because we feel we lack wisdom and perspective, it is here that godly, wise counsel serves us well. A third party can coach us on the facts of the situation. Never be afraid to get input from others when it comes to a choice between two options.

When two choices have merit, we should not be afraid of letting others contribute their perspective on the pros and cons. When we avoid people who are knowledgeable and unbiased, we are stepping over the line and will probably suffer the consequences of our unwillingness to be teachable. For example, I have observed husbands who had a great idea about an investment that was certain to make them rich but they ended up losing heavily. Prior to making this decision, the wife urged him to talk to a couple of men in the church who were financial consultants but he refused.

When we avoid the counsel of others on which course is good and best, we need to ask ourselves why we do not enlist their input. Do we have a selfish agenda and refuse to let anyone point this out? Are we in effect praying, "Not Your will but my will be done"?

For the indecisive personality, when we are following His four wills, we must not lock up when a decision needs to be made between two choices. We must not enter the paralysis of analysis. As long as we are enjoying our relationship with Christ, praising and giving thanks to Him, walking in moral purity, and submitting in doing what is right regardless of the consequences, we will be okay in the eyes of God no matter which way we go, even if this turns out to be the worst decision.

What about those moments that require a permanent decision, like marriage? As Paul said in 1 Corinthians 7:39: "A wife is bound as long as her husband lives." Whereas Joy could move back to L.A. from Portland, she would not be free on a whim to leave the man she married. At the altar we make a vow to remain in the covenant of marriage until death parts us. For this reason, we must seek godly, wise counsel to weigh the pros and cons on what is good and best. Over the years, I have been so impressed with the many folks who came to me as their pastor when asking themselves, "Should I marry this person in the Lord or not?" Some called off the marriage since the good wasn't the best. Others are happily married now after almost forty years because they became aware during counseling that the good was the best.

But what about those daily decisions that are not permanent as such but weigh heavily in importance to us? Take parenting, for example. Daily, our kids put us in positions that demand we go one way or another with them. The good news is that even here we have the freedom to do what seems best. About parents, we read in Hebrews 12:10: "For they disciplined us for a short time as seemed best to them."

Again: "seemed best."

Our parents did not always know which course of action to take. For instance, should they ground us for the weekend or give us grace and not ground us, demonstrating that forgiveness can include absolution? In such instances, God does not write His will in the clouds across the horizon like some aerial skywriting declaring, "Ground the whippersnapper!" Instead, God expects parents to discern and decide based on what "seemed best to them" with that child at this age and stage.

This is subjective, and God expects parents to live in this subjective realm. There is no "thus saith the Lord" on many matters related to our kids. Ironically, this should cause parents to relax. As Sarah and I raised three children, there were many times we were uncertain which way to go, so we had to do what seemed best. However, we took consolation that as we followed the four wills, we were free to follow our conscience and proceed to do what seemed best.

How sad when some parents grow so weary they neglect the four wills of God in their own lives. Feeling defeated as parents, they stop looking to Christ and close Him out because they think He has failed to fulfill His promises to them on parenting. They fight with each other over discipline techniques with the result that they grow to resent each other and stop giving thanks together before God for the trials with the kids. They let the parenting exhaustion and frustration so discourage them that in their defeated state they let down their guard in the marriage itself and end up in an adulterous relationship. And, they stop expecting their child to submit in doing what is right since they lost their moral authority as a parent over their own refusal to submit in doing what is right.

Sarah and I recognized that we had the same vulnerabilities as these parents. However, we made a decision to follow the four wills. Though we were imperfect people and parents, we were committed to looking to Jesus, trusting Him with our parenting even when the kids resisted us. We stayed true to our vow of fidelity to each other knowing that exhaustion from family duties and the feelings of failure could cause a person to push eject on marital faithfulness. We kept returning to the giving of thanks to God during the frustrating moments with our kids because that alone kept us hopeful and positive. And, we submitted in doing what was right as maturely as we could in front of our kids, though in their immaturity they failed to always submit in doing what was right based on our instruction. Over the years, we assured ourselves that if we kept in the center of God's will by doing His four wills, we would make parenting decisions with a clear conscience and could trust our instincts that this was best. We would not be hurting our kids as they observed us humbly looking to Christ, demonstrating a thankful spirit, walking in moral purity, and consistently choosing to do the right thing. Ultimately, we yearned for our kids to act on the four wills and we knew that we needed to exemplify what we expected.

In Possessing the Freedom to Decide, What Attitude Should We Always Have?

Though the apostles taught that they were free to do what seemed good and best, they had a controlling conviction that God had the right to change course at the last minute. They had a deep deferential attitude toward the everyday possibility that the Lord would override their best with His best, their good with His good, and their wishes with His will. God was sovereign. Thus, we hear the writers use language that reflected this yieldedness.

Acts 18:21: "I will return to you again if God wills."

1 Corinthians 4:19: "I will come to you soon, if the Lord wills."

1 Corinthians 16:7: "I hope to remain with you for some time, if the Lord permits."

Hebrews 6:3: "And this we will do, if God permits."

Our omniscient God knows what is wisest and may countermand our conclusions. He can trump our ideas with His ideas and our interests with His interests. We should long for this and always welcome this.

When it came to my daughter Joy moving to Portland from L.A., she needed to keep in mind, as you and I must, that God could close the door to Portland. God is all-knowing and we must have a deferential demeanor toward Him. God has the right to provide new information that makes it clear we ought not to move to Portland. Thus, we must always echo James's instruction:

> Come now, you who say, "Today or tomorrow we will go to such and such a city, and spend a year there and engage in business and make a profit." Yet you do not know what your life will be like tomorrow. You are just a vapor that appears for a little while and then vanishes away. Instead, you ought to say, "If the Lord wills, we will live and also do this or that." (James 4:13–15)

Joy needed to say, "At this point, I am headed to Portland, Lord permitting. The Lord has not revealed otherwise. Because I am obeying His four wills, I believe I am free to move there. However, I am remaining alert to the possibility that God will graciously override this decision and have me remain in L.A. But until I know differently, Lord willing, I am about to become an Oregonian."

That we can relax and do as we please as long as we are doing the four wills of God does not mean we can let down our guard and proceed as though God forfeits His rights to change those plans once we have made up our mind. We should regularly mouth, "Lord willing."

There Is No Absolute Freedom or Autonomy

We must never foolishly believe that we have absolute freedom in directing our own steps. We have been granted a relative freedom based on God's loving permission. God never exits nor forfeits His lordship over us.

We must recognize the mystery here between our autonomy and God's authority, between prerogative and predestination. Both are real. God's controlling presence is wedded to our actions. This is the idea behind Proverbs 16:9, "The mind of man plans his way, but the LORD directs his steps." This is also the prophet's warning in Jeremiah 10:23, "I know, O LORD, that a man's way is not in himself, nor is it in a man who walks to direct his steps."

We must be very cautious in suggesting we can direct our own steps in the sense that we have the final say and God has no authority over us. That would be heresy. He is the Lord and to Him we submit. It is never the other way around.

When we look at all of Scripture, we note that we have the freedom to direct our steps in doing what we wish by doing what seems good and best. When we are uncertain, we have the liberty to make choices. However, we must always trust that God is ever present and moving. We read in Philippians 2:12–13, "work out your salvation with fear and trembling; for it is God who is at work in you, both to will and to work for His good pleasure."

Which is it? Are we working it out or is God working it in?

Yes!

In coming to Christ, we see the sign above the door that says, "Come Whoever Will." We enter, shut the door, and look back and above the doorpost where we read, "Chosen from the Foundation of the World."

Which is it? Did we come or were we chosen?

Yes.

I tell people about the pastor who was an Arminian who believed in total free will and the Dutch Reformed pastor who believed in predestination. Both fell down the steps together as they headed out of the building. As the Arminian stood up he said, "I need to be more careful"; the Reformed pastor stood up and said, "I am glad that's over with."

I recommend we land somewhere in between these two gentlemen—theologically speaking. We refer to this as an antinomy: an apparent contradiction between two doctrines that are in themselves reasonable. However, the contradiction is only apparent to us. God exists in dimensions we cannot imagine. To us it is irrational to argue that both free will and predestination exist, but one day God will remove the blinders.

We have often heard, "Act as though everything depends on you. Believe as though everything depends on God." Though sometimes we have that sense of knowing ahead of a decision that God is speaking to our hearts about His intent, most often we must weigh the pros and cons and do what seems good and best. But we must not get sloppy with our faith and live no differently than an atheist. We need to set our minds on Christ's lordship over our lives. To do this, the four wills serve us well.

Believe Jesus Christ is the Lord of lords.

1 Timothy 6:15: "He who is the blessed and only Sovereign, the King of kings and **Lord of lords**" (emphasis added).

Give thanks to Him as Lord of lords.

Psalm 136:3: "Give thanks to the **Lord of lords**, for His loving-kindness is everlasting" (emphasis added).

Submit to His lordship over us.

1 Peter 2:13: "Submit yourselves for **the Lord's sake** to every human institution, whether to a king as the one in authority" (emphasis added).

Abstain from sexual sin that is incompatible with His lordship.

1 Corinthians 6:13: "Yet the body is not for immorality, but for the Lord, and the Lord is for the body" (CEV translation "the Lord who is in charge of our bodies").

When this is our mind-set, we will be okay. We will not be practical atheists. We will counter the autonomy that most of us feel dominates us more than it ought. As we act on these four, we will demonstrate to God, ourselves, and others that we are yielded to His loving and wise headship.

When we fail and fall, we need to get back up. Proverbs 24:16 says, "a righteous man falls seven times, and rises again."

Is Doing the Universal Will of God Enough for You?

What if humanly, due to any number of reasons, we don't have many good choices? For instance, what if we are thirty years into a job that we do not like and have no feasible way out because we need the pension after retirement? Plus, we are too old to do anything different; no one would hire us even if we wished to launch a new career? Beyond work-related issues, what if we are in prison or have a physical handicap?

This is the power of the four wills. In following them, we can find deep and abiding pleasure in bringing God pleasure. This is the greatest secret of all: finding a degree of happiness knowing we are touching God's heart by doing His will. Our Lord captured this idea when He exclaimed, "My food is to do the will of Him who sent Me" (John 4:34). We can be satisfied and sustained by nourishing ourselves on the four wills, which the rest of this book will reveal. We can stand in place in our prison cell and behold Jesus with the eyes of faith, give Him thanks, keep our heart pure, and follow the prison rules. This pleases God, and the mature person comes to a place where they derive pleasure from pleasing Him. When society or health removes all options from us, these four options always remain.

Mature believers quote the psalmist who sang, "I delight to do Your will, O my God" (Psalm 40:8). Or, we read, "I shall delight in Your commandments, which I love" (Psalm 119:47). Or, "If Your law had not been my delight, then I would have perished in my affliction" (Psalm 119:92).

One great example of God's unique design for a woman with limited opportunities is the daughter of William Booth, founder of the Salvation Army. Though Booth and his wife had several children who eventually held significant positions of leadership in the Salvation Army, their daughter, Marian, contracted smallpox as a child and remained a semi-invalid for life. An introverted woman, Marian simply worked at headquarters and never married. When a friend once said to her, "Marian, it is a pity that a woman of your capabilities should be hindered by sickness from doing the Lord's work," Marian answered, "It's wonderful to do the Lord's work, but it's greater still to do the Lord's will!"[3]

Marian understood what many never grasp: Doing the Lord's will pleases God. The apostle John said that our obedience shows that we "do the things that are pleasing in His sight" (1 John 3:22).

God's Pleasure Is Our Pleasure

I find it fascinating that these four wills do, in fact, please God according to the Bible.

As for believing in God, the writer of Hebrews says, "And without faith it is impossible to **please Him**, for he who comes to God must believe that He is and that He is a rewarder of those who seek Him" (Hebrews 11:6, emphasis added). When we believe in Jesus Christ, we please Him! Each day as we behold the Son with the eyes of faith (John 6:40), we touch the heart of God. For some of us who are locked into a suffocating situation, this can be enough. Chapters 3 and 4 will show you why this is so. And, for those of us who have everything the world has to offer, what difference does that make if we do not please Christ by trusting Him every day of our life?

As for giving thanks in everything (1 Thessalonians 5:18), the writer of Hebrews pens, "let us continually offer up a sacrifice of praise to God, that is, the fruit of lips that give thanks to His name . . . for with such sacrifices **God is pleased**" (Hebrews 13:15–16, emphasis added). When we give thanks in the face of things we do not understand, we affect God's heart. Chapters 5 and 6 make this point.

As for submitting to doing what is right especially before authority (1 Peter 2:13–15), we read in Ephesians 6:6, "not by way of eyeservice, as men-pleasers, but as slaves of Christ, doing the will of God from the heart." Slaves of Christ are Christ pleasers. Chapters 7 and 8 explain how this works.

As for abstaining from sexual sins, Paul writes in 1 Thessalonians 4:1, "you received from us instruction as to how you ought to walk and **please God**" (emphasis added). He then connects pleasing God with sexual purity two verses later in 1 Thessalonians 4:3. Chapters 9 and 10 explain the instruction on how to please God in this way.

By implication, we can find pleasure in pleasing God, and we can help others find this pleasure.

Whatever the unique will of God was for Marian Booth, she found pleasure in pleasing God even if things in her personal life did not unfold as she would normally desire. To her, doing God's will was wonderful in the face of her physical limitations.

My conjecture is that Marian might tell us, "As I beheld and believed in the Son of God, I found peace. As I gave thanks to Him, my heart experienced a gratefulness and a confidence in Him. As I submitted in doing what was right, especially before those in authority over me, I knew my reputation and testimony for the Lord was credible and God would be pleased. As I walked in sexual purity, my conscience was clear and, as Jesus said, I would see God with the eyes of my heart. And, as I helped others apply these precious truths to their lives, my life took on a deep-seated fulfillment."

What If God's Unique Will Entails Tough Times?

At this point, a question arises. Would we want God's will if the Lord called us to do something that we preferred not to do? Given our life was wonderful, what if God revealed His unique will to us that entailed really hard times?

I had my thinking challenged years ago when someone asked me, "Emerson, do you want God's will for your life? Do you want God to work in your life in a powerful way, doing glorious things? Do you want God to really bless you?" I said, "Yes, of course."

The person then said, "Let me ask you another question. If Jesus Christ appeared to you and asked you to do something you didn't want to do, would you do it?"

Before I responded, he said, "And let me say, you can't say, 'I don't know.' If the Son of God, the Savior of the world, the Lord of lords, and the King of kings asked you to do something that you didn't want to do, and you said, 'I don't know,' that is a 'no' answer. Therefore, you can only answer the question with a 'yes' or 'no.'"

I wanted to say, "Yes!" I assume you would too.

Through the years as I've counseled people seeking guidance on God's will, every so often I ask that question: "If Jesus Christ appeared to you and asked you to do something you didn't want to do, would you do it?" Though these folks had come specifically for counsel on God's will, to my surprise, some said, "no."

I recall one fellow saying, "Well, when you put it that way, no, I wouldn't. Why would I? Who in their right mind would do that?"

I proceeded, "I salute you for your honesty. Yet, let me see if I get this straight. You came today because you are seeking God's direction on this particular issue, right? But I just asked you, 'If Jesus Christ appeared to you, and asked you to do something you didn't want to do, you would tell Him 'No'?"

"Yes, I said, 'no.'"

"Forgive me if I'm wrong," I continued, "but it appears that you don't want *God's* will. It appears to me that you want God to do *your* will. You're here because you want Him to fulfill your wishes. In fact, you want me to affirm those desires. Could it be that you are reversing one of the best-known prayers of Jesus? Jesus prayed, 'Yet not as I will, but as You will' (Matthew 26:39). You are praying, "Yet not as You will, but as I will.""

I added, "If today I share truth from the Bible about God's will on the matter before you and that truth runs contrary to your wishes, is it safe to say that you won't follow based on what you just told me?"

Silence usually follows this question, as it did with this gentleman. People don't want to admit it, but when pushed to consider their words, they can see that my line of questioning exposes conflicts in their desire to follow God's will.

What's going on here? These folks have a hidden and probably selfish agenda that intends (maybe subconsciously) to manipulate God. They want me to tell them that God sanctions their desires. However, they also know that if I tell them something they do not want to hear, they will simply go to someone who will give counsel to confer with their own desires.

How often do we employ the same tactic? Years ago a young Christian woman came to me for counseling. She intended to divorce her husband and wanted me to help her step through the process of her divorce. Obviously, I needed to know more information. I asked if her husband had committed adultery, deserted her, beat her, or demonstrated bad will to her. "No," she replied with a measure of irritation.

"Does your husband want to live with you and be married to you?" I requested. "Yes!" she shouted. "Why are you asking me all these questions?" I explained, "You do not have biblical grounds for divorce, and you don't even have social reasons for a physical separation. I am curious, what are your reasons?"

Infuriated, she said, "Look, God wants me to be happy, and I'm not happy in this marriage. I don't want to be married to this man. I want my freedom."

Surprised by her candor, I said, "Well, I need to tell you that in the eyes of God, you are married to this man until death, and God does not sanction you divorcing him."

How did she respond? How do so many of us respond when we stare clearly at the will of God? She said, "Well, I'll just go down the street and meet with a minister who will tell me what I want to hear."

Isn't this what we all do at some time in our relationship with God when we square into a principle we don't like? Don't we try to find a book, a friend, a teacher, or a philosophy that supports what we want to hear? This woman wasn't seeking counsel; she was seeking approval for her plan. Is this not an example of Paul's description of many in the last days who "will not endure sound doctrine; but wanting to have their ears tickled, they will accumulate for themselves teachers in accordance to their own desires" (2 Timothy 4:3)?

Do some of our prayers to God reflect this same maneuver?

If we really want to know God's unique will for our life, quite simply, we must begin by laying down our own plans and listening to Him, especially when we know that our plans contradict the clear instructions of God in the Bible. We cannot approach the throne of God with our petitions if all we expect God to do is "rubberstamp" our agenda. He doesn't operate this way. So, let me ask you, if Jesus Christ appeared to you and asked you to do what you did not want to do, would you say "yes" or "no"?

You and I want to say "yes," but how can we know if we would say "yes"? First John 3:21–22 gives us a clue: "Beloved, if our heart does not condemn us, we have confidence before God; and whatever we ask we receive from Him, because we keep His commandments and do the things that are pleasing in His sight."

The clue is, "because we keep His commandments." Only if we are keeping God's commandments (and the four wills are part of these universal commands) will we receive unique answers from Him. This is why I promote the idea of starting here with the four, otherwise we might feel overwhelmed by all of God's commandments.

How can we be sure that obedience to the commands is a necessary premise to receiving His unique answers for us? Let me answer that question with a question. Would God reveal His unique will to you if you did not intend to follow that unique will and His universal will? While we cannot fully know the mind of God, it doesn't seem likely. So notice what the person in 1 John 3:22 does in order to experience and follow God's unique will: he keeps God's commands.

Keeping God's commands is the key to asking and receiving from God. The good news is that if you are already saying "yes" to God's universal will, you will say "yes" to God's unique will no matter what it entails. But when you distrust and disregard the universal will, then wanting God's unique will is suspect.

"But," you may ask, "how can I really know I would follow His unique will if it entailed things I don't like? Might I say 'no' to God?" If you are saying "yes" to God's universal will, and that requires doing what you don't always like, you will say "yes" to God's unique will even if it includes things you don't like.

Bottom line: when you do the universal will of God, you will have no trouble doing His unique will. So, if you want to learn God's will regarding specific choices about any specific issue, such as a career, a move, a relationship, or a potential spouse, then *start* by checking to see if you are rightly aligned to God by following the basic commands He lays out in the four passages that state, "This is the will of God." And, if you are not ignoring these four then you can know—you can have the confidence—that you truly want God's unique will and will do it, even if it includes tough times.

———

Are you ready to dive into the four universal wills of God, discussing all they entail and how they relate to God's unique will for your life? Me too. In the chapters ahead, we'll spend plenty of time learning all it means to 1) believe in Jesus Christ, 2) give thanks in everything, 3) submit in doing right, and 4) abstain from sexual sin.

But before we do, let's take a short self-evaluation so that you can best know where you're starting from. Just as God's will for each of us is unique, so are our current strengths and weaknesses. Take a few moments now to learn more about where you are currently as it pertains to the four universal wills.

— Are You Doing the Four Wills of God? An Evaluation —

Agree/Disagree

Please respond to the following statements by circling the number that identifies with your response to each statement:

Answer key: 1 = strongly agree, 2 = somewhat agree, 3 = undecided, 4 = somewhat disagree, 5 = strongly disagree, N/A = not applicable

A. I have a desire to find and do God's will for my life.

1 = strongly agree, 2 = somewhat agree, 3 = undecided, 4 = somewhat disagree, 5 = strongly disagree, N/A = not applicable

B. I am seeking to grow in my faith.

1 = strongly agree, 2 = somewhat agree, 3 = undecided, 4 = somewhat disagree, 5 = strongly disagree, N/A = not applicable

C. I am thankful to God for the challenges He has placed in my life.

1 = strongly agree, 2 = somewhat agree, 3 = undecided, 4 = somewhat disagree, 5 = strongly disagree, N/A = not applicable

D. I am able to resist sexual temptations.

1 = strongly agree, 2 = somewhat agree, 3 = undecided, 4 = somewhat disagree, 5 = strongly disagree, N/A = not applicable

E. I have an easy time trusting just and honorable authority.

1 = strongly agree, 2 = somewhat agree, 3 = undecided, 4 = somewhat disagree, 5 = strongly disagree, N/A = not applicable

F. I believe God has my best interest at heart.

1 = strongly agree, 2 = somewhat agree, 3 = undecided, 4 = somewhat disagree, 5 = strongly disagree, N/A = not applicable

G. I thank God for my spouse and family.

1 = strongly agree, 2 = somewhat agree, 3 = undecided, 4 = somewhat disagree, 5 = strongly disagree, N/A = not applicable

H. I agree with the biblical principle of submitting to authority.

1 = strongly agree, 2 = somewhat agree, 3 = undecided, 4 = somewhat disagree, 5 = strongly disagree, N/A = not applicable

I. I have learned how to control my sexual appetite.

1 = strongly agree, 2 = somewhat agree, 3 = undecided, 4 = somewhat disagree, 5 = strongly disagree, N/A = not applicable

J. Trusting God has not been difficult for me.

1 = strongly agree, 2 = somewhat agree, 3 = undecided, 4 = somewhat disagree, 5 = strongly disagree, N/A = not applicable

K. I have never resented God for the difficulties that have come my way.

1 = strongly agree, 2 = somewhat agree, 3 = undecided, 4 = somewhat disagree, 5 = strongly disagree, N/A = not applicable

L. I have no regrets related to past sexual experiences.

1 = strongly agree, 2 = somewhat agree, 3 = undecided, 4 = somewhat disagree, 5 = strongly disagree, N/A = not applicable

M. I have placed my faith in Jesus Christ for the forgiveness of my sins.

1 = strongly agree, 2 = somewhat agree, 3 = undecided, 4 = somewhat disagree, 5 = strongly disagree, N/A = not applicable

N. When there is suffering in my life, I give thanks to God regardless.

1 = strongly agree, 2 = somewhat agree, 3 = undecided, 4 = somewhat disagree, 5 = strongly disagree, N/A = not applicable

O. I consider myself to be a person who knows how to submit to authority.

1 = strongly agree, 2 = somewhat agree, 3 = undecided, 4 = somewhat disagree, 5 = strongly disagree, N/A = not applicable

P. I have healthy attitudes regarding my sexual behavior.

1 = strongly agree, 2 = somewhat agree, 3 = undecided, 4 = somewhat disagree, 5 = strongly disagree, N/A = not applicable

Q. I try to be strong in my faith in God every day.

1 = strongly agree, 2 = somewhat agree, 3 = undecided, 4 = somewhat disagree, 5 = strongly disagree, N/A = not applicable

R. It is my routine to "be thankful" in everything.

1 = strongly agree, 2 = somewhat agree, 3 = undecided, 4 = somewhat disagree, 5 = strongly disagree, N/A = not applicable

S. Under authority figures, I submit to doing what is right.

1 = strongly agree, 2 = somewhat agree, 3 = undecided, 4 = somewhat disagree, 5 = strongly disagree, N/A = not applicable

T. Overall, I have a positive attitude about my sexual life.

1 = strongly agree, 2 = somewhat agree, 3 = undecided, 4 = somewhat disagree, 5 = strongly disagree, N/A = not applicable

U. I believe God has a unique plan for my life.

1 = strongly agree, 2 = somewhat agree, 3 = undecided, 4 = somewhat disagree, 5 = strongly disagree, N/A = not applicable

V. I believe Jesus Christ is the way to God and eternal life.

1 = strongly agree, 2 = somewhat agree, 3 = undecided, 4 = somewhat disagree, 5 = strongly disagree, N/A = not applicable

W. The will of God is clearly stated in the Bible.

1 = strongly agree, 2 = somewhat agree, 3 = undecided, 4 = somewhat disagree, 5 = strongly disagree, N/A = not applicable

X. If God Himself appeared to me and asked me to do what I did not want to do, I would do it.

1 = strongly agree, 2 = somewhat agree, 3 = undecided, 4 = somewhat disagree, 5 = strongly disagree, N/A = not applicable

Y. I respectfully do what is rightfully required of me by those over me.

1 = strongly agree, 2 = somewhat agree, 3 = undecided, 4 = somewhat disagree, 5 = strongly disagree, N/A = not applicable

Z. I do not worry about missing God's unique will for my life.

1 = strongly agree, 2 = somewhat agree, 3 = undecided, 4 = somewhat disagree, 5 = strongly disagree, N/A = not applicable

AA. I have no major doubts about the Bible or questions about my faith.

1 = strongly agree, 2 = somewhat agree, 3 = undecided, 4 = somewhat disagree, 5 = strongly disagree, N/A = not applicable

BB. I am thankful in and for everything since God works all things together for good.

1 = strongly agree, 2 = somewhat agree, 3 = undecided, 4 = somewhat disagree, 5 = strongly disagree, N/A = not applicable

CC. I never rebel when asked to do what is right, even though it is an inconvenience.

1 = strongly agree, 2 = somewhat agree, 3 = undecided, 4 = somewhat disagree, 5 = strongly disagree, N/A = not applicable

DD. I do not struggle with being sexually pure.

1 = strongly agree, 2 = somewhat agree, 3 = undecided, 4 = somewhat disagree, 5 = strongly disagree, N/A = not applicable

EE. I know that Christ is in me and loves me, and this makes me feel valued.

1 = strongly agree, 2 = somewhat agree, 3 = undecided, 4 = somewhat disagree, 5 = strongly disagree, N/A = not applicable

FF. Since I believe Christ died for me, I know God accepts me forevermore.

1 = strongly agree, 2 = somewhat agree, 3 = undecided, 4 = somewhat disagree, 5 = strongly disagree, N/A = not applicable

GG. I know the Lord is in me and will never leave or forsake me.

1 = strongly agree, 2 = somewhat agree, 3 = undecided, 4 = somewhat disagree, 5 = strongly disagree, N/A = not applicable

If you have answered 10 or more with 3 = undecided, 4 = somewhat disagree, 5 = strongly disagree, N/A = not applicable, then this book is for you! You need to be applauded for your honest self-assessment. This book addresses the concerns raised by these issues. Each chapter can serve you in your spiritual journey in finding and doing the will of God for your life.

If you have answered nearly 100 percent with 1 = strongly agree, 2 = somewhat agree, then this book echoes your knowledge of God's will and your willingness to follow His will. This book can serve as a resource for you in helping other people discover what you have discovered. Please use this book in small groups or one-on-one to assist others in finding God's unique will for their lives.

After taking the survey above, mark the letter there and below that represents the areas you believe you need to address and improve. Take a look at the several clusters below and read the book with them in mind.

Clusters in Five Areas

The Will of God

A: I have a desire to find and do God's will for my life.

U: I believe God has a unique plan for my life.

W: The will of God is clearly stated in the Bible.

X: If God Himself appeared to me and asked me to do what I did not want to do, I would do it.

Z: I do not worry about missing God's unique will for my life.

AA: I have no major doubts about the Bible or questions about my faith.

Believing in Jesus Christ

B: I am seeking to grow in my faith.

F: I believe God has my best interest at heart.

J: Trusting God has not been difficult for me.

M: I have placed my faith in Jesus Christ for the forgiveness of my sins.

Q: I try to be strong in my faith in God every day.

V: I believe Jesus Christ is the way to God and eternal life.

EE: I know that Christ is in me and loves me, and this makes me feel valued.

FF: Since I believe Christ died for me, I know God accepts me forevermore.

GG: I know the Lord is in me and will never leave or forsake me.

Giving Thanks in Everything

C: I am thankful to God for the challenges He has placed in my life.

G: I thank God for my spouse and family.

K: I have never resented God for the difficulties that have come my way.

N: When there is suffering in my life, I give thanks to God regardless.

R: It is my routine to "be thankful" in everything.

BB: I am thankful in and for everything since God works all things together for good.

Submitting to Doing Right

E: I have an easy time trusting just and honorable authority.

H: I agree with the biblical principle of submitting to authority.

O: I consider myself to be a person who knows how to submit to authority.

S: Under authority figures, I submit to doing what is right.

Y: I respectfully do what is rightfully required of me by those over me.

CC: I never rebel when asked to do what is right, even though it is an inconvenience.

Abstaining from Sexual Sin

> D: I am able to resist sexual temptations.
>
> I: I have learned how to control my sexual appetite.
>
> L: I have no regrets related to past sexual experiences.
>
> P: I have healthy attitudes regarding my sexual behavior.
>
> T: Overall, I have a positive attitude about my sexual life.
>
> DD: I do not struggle with being sexually pure.

First, Read the Will That Speaks Most to Your Heart

Based on the cluster most challenging to you, please consider turning first to those two chapters addressing that topic. Though you need to follow all four wills, you may be going through a season where God is speaking to you about one of these. Thus, feel free to read the following chapters in any order you desire.

If you are not sure of what you believe about Jesus Christ, or what an active faith in Him should look like, then by all means begin with chapters 3 and 4. Certainly believing in Jesus Christ is central to following the other three wills, so make sure you understand what Jesus meant when He said, "This is the will of My Father" (John 6:40).

If you are sure of your relationship to Christ and who you are in Him, you may want to begin with one of the other chapters. Each considers an aspect of our lives that affects our ability to discern God's unique will for us.

Chapters 5 and 6 deal with our attitudes. Are you filled with gratitude for your life or too often filled with anger, anxiety, or fear? This chapter on giving thanks shows how attitudes of our hearts and minds open doors for God to lead you to His unique will.

Chapters 7 and 8 deal with our relationships to those who have authority over us about doing what is right in those settings. How do your responses to your "bosses" shape your ability to find God's unique plans for you? Or, how do you conduct yourself when you know what the right thing is to do but it is easier to submit to doing what is wrong?

Chapters 9 and 10 deal with our bodies. Are you willing to consider God's view of sexuality? These chapters call you to consider how the purity of your mind and body influences your ability to learn God's purposes for you.

No matter where you read, if you desire to live the adventure of faith that leads you to God's unique will for you, these four wills enable this.

Chapter 3
GOD'S WILL: BELIEVE IN
JESUS CHRIST

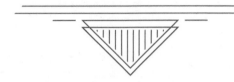

"This Is the Will of My Father . . ."

The first of the four wills to address, and the one that should precede the other three, is stated by Jesus. In John 6:40, He declares the very heart of the Christian message: "This is the will of My Father that everyone who beholds the Son and believes in Him will have eternal life, and I Myself will raise him up on the last day."

Is there any other announcement so glorious and full of hope and excitement? Think about it. Jesus tells us that God His Father wants us to know Him, and that He, Jesus, will give us eternal life!

Eternal life is God's will, and the means for receiving such life is to believe in the Son of God!

Do you believe this? No question holds more power over your destiny than this.

If you desire to know God's will, you must first know God. Knowing God, according to John 6:40, begins by believing that Jesus is the one and only Son of God. The certainty and exclusivity of this claim unsettled the Hebrew world of the first century. It continues to do so.

While the Hebrews first called Christ a fraud and blasphemer, reasons to deny the message of Christ have multiplied over the centuries. Focus on scientific discoveries, philosophical reasoning, psychology, and the claims of other global religions have led to attacks on the authenticity and exclusivity of Christianity and religious belief at large. Be it atheists, agnostics, existentialists, moral relativists, or believers in other religions—the case against faith in Christ generally boils down to one of the following claims:

- There is no God.
- There is no way to know what to believe and no right way to believe.
- All that we know is that we can't know anything for sure.
- All religions are paths to God.
- God is a psychological crutch made by men to fulfill their needs.
- Jesus is not God's Son, the Savior and Lord.

I won't engage these objections other than to quote Jesus who comforts me, and I hope you, on each of these sincere objections. "This is the will of My Father that everyone who beholds the Son and believes in Him will have eternal life, and I Myself will raise him up on the last day."

> *According to Jesus, the Father is there.*
>
> *According to Jesus, we can know what to believe and there is a right way to believe.*
>
> *According to Jesus, we can know that believing in Him is the will of His Father.*
>
> *According to Jesus, believing in Him is the way to eternal life.*
>
> *According to Jesus, trusting Him is not a trick and a crutch.*
>
> *According to Jesus, He is God's Son with unique authority to raise the dead.*

This chapter explores the claims of Christ that lead to a personal relationship with God. To Jesus, there is sufficient reason and evidence to trust Him. If anyone is worthy of our trust, Jesus Christ is. He was and is the perfect gentleman. Let's trust His words.

To those of you considering what to believe about Jesus Christ, the verses that follow explain God's gift of new life through His Son, Jesus. My question to you as you read these truths is: Will you choose to believe them?

If you already know Jesus as your personal Savior, the truths of this chapter are the foundation of your faith. As you read and review them, ask yourself: Are you fully invested in what you say you believe? Have you let the power of these promises take root in all the choices you make?

Believe and Receive

Seeking God's unique will for your life begins by trusting Jesus as your Savior and then learning to let Him lead you as a shepherd. As John wrote, "And whatever we ask we receive from Him, because we keep His commandments and do the things that are pleasing in His sight. This is His commandment, that we believe in the name of His Son Jesus Christ . . ." (1 John 3:22–23).

Obviously, and generally speaking, God will not reveal His unique will to those who do not believe in Him or to those who have created their own version of Him. Thus, the first will asks us to "behold the Son and believe in Him."

But, what does this really mean? What are you asked to behold and believe in John 6:40? Though bumper stickers and ball field posters boldly declare the good news of John 3:16, consider again this amazing truth: "For God so loved the world, that He gave His only begotten Son, that whoever believes in Him will not perish, but have eternal life."

Recently my six-year-old grandson, Jackson, learned John 3:16 in Sunday school. He was asked about this verse by his mom and dad and he replied, "It just makes sense."

I hope you discover the same as I address this issue of believing in the "only begotten Son."

What are we to believe?

We begin by believing God loves us enough to sacrifice His only Son. Incredible! But look at what else you are asked to believe as you consider other promises in the New Testament:

You receive eternal life.

> "Truly, truly, I say to you, he who believes has eternal life." (John 6:47)

God will keep you for Himself forever.

> "And I give eternal life to them, and they will never perish; and no one will snatch them out of My hand." (John 10:28)

You will be changed to His likeness on the last day.

> "In a moment, in the twinkling of an eye, at the last trumpet . . . the dead will be raised imperishable, and we will be changed." (1 Corinthians 15:52)

Christ Himself will come to take you home.

> "For the Lord Himself will descend from heaven with a shout, with the voice of the archangel and with the trumpet of God, and the dead in Christ will rise first." (1 Thessalonians 4:16)

You will share an eternity of indescribable beauty, delight, and happiness.

> "Today you shall be with Me in Paradise" (The words that Jesus told the forgiven man nailed on the adjacent cross in Luke 23:43).

You will be filled with joy as you stand blameless in God's glorious presence.

> We will be "revealed with Him in glory" (Colossians 3:4) and "stand in the presence of His glory blameless with great joy" (Jude 24) as we experience "an eternal weight of glory far beyond all comparison" (2 Corinthians 4:17; see Romans 8:18).

Oh the joy of knowing that Christ Jesus promises us a forever glory! Indeed, we will live happily ever after with Him.

Who Is the Son?

"Happily ever after" is not just the stuff of fairy tales. God put that longing in the heart of every one of us—to be happy forever. It is the promise of God's Word for all who believe in His Son. And, it conveys the uniqueness of Christianity. What great leader besides Jesus ever made a profession and pledge about granting eternal life? Who else has been able to convince half the world to believe it? No wonder the early followers called this message the "gospel," or good news!

When I first understood Jesus' promise of eternal life, I wept. It registered with me that God loves me and forgives me, and that my life on Earth is not the end of the story. The essential truths of the Bible that I chose to believe when I committed my life to Him were the following: Jesus, God's Son, came to Earth in the likeness of man—called the Incarnation—with the goal of taking the sin of the world upon Himself as God's ultimate sacrificial lamb. Because He suffered the punishment for my sins, paying the price to make me right in the eyes of God, I became God's forgiven child.

To make this commitment, I believed that Jesus was:

- The incarnate One—God in human flesh

  John 1:14: "And the Word became flesh, and dwelt among us."

- The Son of the Most High

  Luke 1:31–32: "You will conceive in your womb and bear a son, and you shall name Him Jesus. He will be great and will be called the Son of the Most High."

- The sinless One

  2 Corinthians 5:21: "He made Him who knew no sin to be sin on our behalf, so that we might become the righteousness of God in Him."

- The sacrificial lamb

  Matthew 26:28: "For this is My blood of the covenant, which is poured out for many for forgiveness of sins."

  Revelation 7:14: "Made . . . white in the blood of the Lamb."

- The One who paid the ransom

  Matthew 20:28: "Just as the Son of Man did not come to be served, but to serve, and to give His life a ransom for many."

- The Lord of lords and King of kings

  Revelation 17:14: "The Lamb will overcome them, because He is Lord of lords and King of kings."

Reading these verses, and scores of others that describe who Jesus is, not just what He taught, I realized what the writers intended: Jesus Himself is the focus. This was about who He was, and less so about His moral teachings. As many of us have heard, "He was more than a carpenter." He said that He guaranteed life after death. As John 6:40 declares, "This is the will of My Father that everyone who beholds the Son and believes in Him will have eternal life and I Myself will raise him up on the last day."

I believed, and the longer I live the more it makes sense, as my six-year-old grandson said. However, for many years I did not understand this, and neither did Bernhard Langer.

He Is Resurrected!

I once stayed in the home of Bernhard Langer, two-time winner of the Masters, one of the PGA Tour's four major tournaments. As a result of the positive effect my Love and Respect ministry had on their marriage, he and his wife, Vikki, asked me to spend several days at their home, and during that time, he shared his personal story with me.

In 1985 when he won the Masters for the first time at Augusta, Georgia, the announcers ushered him into the infamous cabin where one of them asked him, "Did you look at the leader board?" Bernhard replied, "I was trying not to look, but I saw it for the first time at the ninth; and I thought, 'Jesus Christ, I am playing well, and I am four shots behind!'"

Using the Lord's name in vain prompted hundreds of people to write him letters complaining to him about such language. At that time, he had no idea what it meant to have a personal relationship with Jesus Christ. To him using Christ's name was a mere expression, not a curse. Though he considered himself a believer, because he was raised in church and had served as an altar boy, he admits he didn't understand the message of the New Testament. In his book, *Bernhard Langer: My Autobiography,* he writes, "I always thought just being a good person and keeping the commandments would hopefully get me to heaven. I didn't steal or kill and tried not to hurt anyone on purpose. As I got more and more successful, I thought I could do it all myself."[1] Fortunately, several days after winning the Masters, he was invited to a PGA Bible study and heard Larry Moody explain the gospel message. Bernhard comments, "I was amazed to realize that the only way to have eternal life was through Jesus Christ—that he died for our sins. And that it was not through worthy deeds or good behavior that one received eternal life, because we can never live up to God's standard. We will always fall short."[2]

Interestingly, eight years after his first Masters championship, he won the tournament again. "The 1993 Masters finished on Easter Sunday. . . . The first question I was asked was how the first Masters' win compared with the second. I answered, 'It's a great honor to win the greatest tournament in the world, and especially on Easter Sunday, the day my Lord was resurrected.' In saying those words, which went round the world on live television, I hope I was able to make up for my shortcomings in 1985 by saying something more positive. Having the opportunity of sharing with the world my faith in Jesus Christ was, for me, a unique situation . . . you see, I strongly believe that the resurrection of Jesus actually happened."[3]

Jesus said in Matthew 7:21, "Not everyone who says to me, 'Lord, Lord,' will enter the kingdom of heaven, but he who does the will of My Father who is in heaven will enter." What is the first and foremost will of the Father for us to do? According to John 6:40, one must believe in Jesus Christ His Son. Bernhard Langer finally understood this. Do you?

The Bad News and the Good News

As humans, we have a dilemma. On the one hand the Bible says in Galatians 3:10, "Cursed is everyone who does not abide by all things written in the book of the law, to perform them." In other words, God's standard is a perfect performance. We must obey all of His commands, all the time. When we sin in one tiny way, we flunk the whole test. The apostle James says, "For whoever keeps the whole law and yet stumbles in one point, he has become guilty of all" (James 2:10). Though many good and basically moral folks contend, "I sincerely did more good than bad," such moral relativism falls short of God's requirement for perfection.

On the other hand, Galatians 3:13 provides us with good news. There we learn, "Christ redeemed us from the curse of the Law, having become a curse for us—for it is written, 'Cursed is everyone who hangs on a tree.'" When Jesus went to the cross, His action rescued and ransomed us from eternal separation from God. In short, Jesus Christ paid the penalty for what we did wrong. Thus, He has the divine right to declare, "I Myself will raise him up on the last day" (John 6:40).

Those who reject Christ, and this saddens me beyond imagination, "will pay the penalty of eternal destruction, away from the presence of the Lord and from the glory of His power" (2 Thessalonians 1:9). If we do not let Jesus Christ pay the penalty for our sins, we will pay the penalty. That penalty entails abandonment forever from the presence and glory of Abba Father. But, for the believer, God provides overwhelmingly good news! Jesus, "having forgiven us all our transgressions," has "canceled out the certificate of debt" (Colossians 2:13–14).

Do you understand this message? In applying this to God's guidance of your life, you cannot ignore this universal will of God and expect to receive personal guidance from Him. Yes, God shows love and kindness to all of us at various stages (Luke 6:35; Acts 14:17) but to receive eternal life, Jesus is clear: believe in Him.

The beautiful thing is that when you receive Him as your Lord, Jesus then becomes not only your Savior, but He also becomes your shepherd. As shepherd, Jesus promises to lead and guide you in a relationship of deep personal intimacy. For the one who chooses to believe, Jesus says, "To him the doorkeeper opens, and the sheep hear his voice, and he calls his own sheep by name and leads them out" (John 10:3). They follow because they personally know His voice! And, they follow because He calls them by name! Extraordinarily, we have a personal relationship with God! Some mock the idea as presumptuous that we can know God in this way but not Jesus.

God Does Not Grade on a Curve

Some do not pay attention to Jesus' claims, though they will tell you that they believe in Jesus. They have a nominal affiliation with a church, Jesus' bride, and see themselves as Christians. I have asked the following question of hundreds of such folks, "If you were to die tonight and were to stand before the Lord, and the Lord asked you why He should let you in to heaven, what would you say to Him?" Many people answer, "I would tell Him that I have sincerely tried to do more good than bad."

This response compels me to ask, "Who is Jesus Christ to you? What difference does Jesus Christ make concerning your eternal destiny?" Though some of these folks will acknowledge that Jesus came to pay for sin, they essentially believe in their own goodness. To focus this, I say, "Based on the answer to your first question, you don't need Jesus Christ to get you into heaven. To you, getting into heaven is a result of you sincerely doing good works. From what you said, Jesus Christ did not need to die on the cross for your sins because it's your sincerity and good works that gains heaven for you." As the apostle Paul wrote in Galatians 2:21, ". . . if righteousness comes through the Law, then Christ died needlessly."

Many of these folks drop their mouths open in surprise. For the first time they get it. They detect that they have not fully taken in that Jesus Christ was crucified (today's version might be the electric chair), for all the crimes they committed against God's laws. Instead, they believe God grades on a curve. Because they think they are better than most people and have done more good than bad, God will accept them into heaven. Not until they are asked to explain the source of their belief do they unearth that they have put their trust in their own efforts. Until this moment, Jesus' sacrifice on the cross was unnecessary.

How sad that many of these good folks miss the whole point, and thus do not experience God's personal presence and power.

Triggering His Presence and Power

Many choose to hover near Christianity for years without comprehending John 6:40 and the other Scriptures we just read. Larry Johnson, a friend of mine from Cedar Rapids, Iowa, is a perfect example. In his first fourteen years of ministry as an associate pastor at a Presbyterian church, he focused solely on the concerns of the social gospel—helping the poor and dealing with issues of justice. Claiming that professors at the liberal seminary he attended had destroyed his personal faith in Jesus Christ, he had spent fourteen years in ministry trying to "do good," but not believing that God was personable, powerful, or present. God, he had been taught, exited the world after creating it.

One afternoon all of that changed. On the beach with his daughter, Larry observed a car rolling down the dune toward his girl. He could not get to her quickly enough to pull her out of the way. All he could do while running toward her was watch in horror as the car knocked her down and rolled over her head. But, as he ran, he cried out, "Oh God, help me!"

When he got her to the hospital, the doctors told him there was a million to one chance that internal bleeding would not begin. If bleeding commenced, she could be in serious trouble. After days of dreading she would bleed into her brain, they recognized, to everyone's surprise, that she had been spared. Other than experiencing recurrent nightmares, she fully recovered.

Later, Larry wondered why he had cried out to God on the beach. If God did not exist in the world, what prompted him to call out to Him in crisis? Desperate for answers, he picked up the Bible and re-read the teaching of Jesus in the Gospels. He beheld the Son! When he began reading, he knew "about" Christ: he did not know Christ personally. As he read, his eyes were opened to the reality of Christ. He watched Jesus model faith in His heavenly Father as He did miraculous deeds. The Jesus of the Gospels was very much personable, powerful, and present!

As he continued to read the Word, Larry decided to write down the many promises of Jesus. When he read, "Come to Me, all who are weary and heavy-laden, and I will give you rest" (Matthew 11:28), Larry decided to ask Christ to take over his life and forgive him of his sins. For the first time in his life, he acted and believed as though everything Jesus did and said was true. He decided that for six months he would trust in these promises. If they did not work, he would leave the ministry. If they did work, well, he'd stay in the ministry and change the way he pastored.

According to Larry, what happened was nothing short of miraculous. He began telling people about Jesus and called them to place their faith in Him. As he prayed with people and instructed them to ask Jesus to forgive them, he experienced in these six months more dramatic changes in the lives of scores of people than in all fourteen years of his social justice ministry.

Larry followed this universal will of God about believing in Jesus and it triggered Larry's experience of God's unique will for his life.

When Larry and I met, and then started the Open Door Counseling Center, he told me that he would first and foremost go over the gospel with each person. Since he had spent years forfeiting the personal presence and power of the Lord, he determined that he would not deprive people of the joy and peace he found in knowing Christ personally. As Jesus said, "I am the good shepherd, and I know My own and My own know Me, even as the Father knows Me and I know the Father" (John 10:14–15).

This raises the question, "Can a person conclude that he or she is a believer in Jesus Christ when in fact they are not?" The apostle Paul addresses this very issue when he said, "Test yourselves to see if you are in the faith; examine yourselves! Or do you not recognize this about yourselves, that Jesus

Christ is in you?" (2 Corinthians 13:5). Paul acknowledges that a person can be self-deceived, or be ignorant about how to receive Christ into one's heart.

I have met many people like Larry Johnson and Bernhard Langer who know about Jesus but have never heard what I am about to say to you concerning the importance of asking Jesus Christ to come into your heart. Please read carefully. If you've never understood this, you are about to change forever because of what the Bible says.

Some Life-Defining Questions about Jesus Christ

Let me ask you a few questions. To begin, do you recall a time that you said, "I believe in You, Jesus Christ, and I ask You to come into me"? If not, look at 1 John 5:11–13 below and permit me to ask several questions. "And the testimony is this, that God has given us eternal life, and this life is in His Son. He who has the Son has the life; he who does not have the Son of God does not have the life. These things I have written to you who believe in the name of the Son of God, so that you may know that you have eternal life."

Based on the above verses from 1 John 5:11–13, consider carefully your response to the following commonly asked questions:

Can you know if you have eternal life?

Many people believe it is not possible to know if they have eternal life. But consider John's certainty in 1 John 5:13, "These things I have written to you who believe in the name of the Son of God, so that you may *know* that you have eternal life." John is clear: "you may *know* that you have eternal life."

How can you know if you have eternal life?

Read 1 John 5:12 again: "He who has the Son has the life; he who does not have the Son of God does not have the life." You can know that you have eternal life if you "have" the Son of God.

How do you "have" the Son of God to have eternal life?

Turning to John's Gospel, we read in John 1:12, "But as many as received Him, to them He gave the right to become children of God, even to those who believe in His name." Simply put, you must receive Jesus Christ to "have the Son of God."

What does receiving Jesus Christ look like?

It is as simple as asking Jesus to come inside you, to indwell you, to live in you by His Spirit. By childlike faith you invite Him in. Jesus said in John 14:20 that He will be "in you." The apostle Paul writes in Romans 8:9, "If anyone does not have the Spirit of Christ, he does not belong to Him." This is why he appealed to the Corinthians to make sure that Jesus was "in" them (2 Corinthians 13:5).

Have you asked Jesus to be your Savior?

To "have the Son" and gain eternal life, you must ask Jesus Christ to come into you. Have you?

> If you have not, would you pray right now and invite Jesus Christ to take up residence within you by His Spirit?

Pray This Prayer

"Father God I believe You are there. I believe Jesus Christ is Your Son. I understand that Jesus Christ died on the cross for my sin. I recognize that I must ask You to forgive me for my sins based on Christ's sacrificial death for me, so that when I die, my sins will not keep me out of heaven. Though I deserve eternal separation from You, by believing in the Son I will receive eternal life. I receive this gift of grace because Jesus paid the penalty for my wrongdoing. Thank You. Spirit of Christ, come into me and take up residence in me. Live Your life in me."

When you sincerely pray this prayer, not only do you receive eternal life, you receive the Spirit of Christ to live in you. Unique and personal things start happening. Whether you have just put your trust in Jesus or you have been a believer for years, the fact that you chose to follow the first of the four universal wills—to "believe in Him" (John 6:40)—puts you in relationship to know God's unique will for you.

Trust that the Lord Jesus can sustain and satisfy your soul in whatever circumstances you face. He said, "he who believes in Me will never thirst" (John 6:35) and "he who believes in Me, as the Scripture said, 'From his innermost being will flow rivers of living water'" (John 7:38). When you follow this universal will, you will encounter the unique indwelling Christ. Expect to personally and uniquely experience the Spirit's presence, peace, purpose, and power. More than having your steps personally directed to this job or city, some of you will declare with delight, "Christ's indwelling; this is enough!"

But let's go a bit deeper into two truths that can revolutionize your life. We will answer the question, *What does it mean on a daily basis for Christ to be in you?* And added to this, *What does it mean for you who are "in Christ"?*

Chapter 4
YOU IN CHRIST AND CHRIST IN YOU

When you received Christ, you received eternal life. But something else transpired. I will share two truths that changed me, and still are. I am in process. Jesus captures these two ideas when He says in John 14:20, "you in Me, and I in you." Again in John 15:4 He says, "Abide in Me, and I in you."

This raises the question: What does it mean for you to be in Christ and Christ in you?

This is important because there will come moments of questioning. Back in 2003, at age fifty-one, I wrote in my journal, "For me, twenty-seven years ago, at age twenty-five, I decided to wait on God for twenty-five years before I authored a book. In my mind's eye, I envisioned at age fifty a national ministry. Well, fifty has come and gone. I am now fifty-one. Unlike Henry Blackaby, a friend and author of *Experiencing God*, who has five thousand requests to speak, I have none on the table at present. This doesn't sound like a national ministry to me because it isn't. What I envisioned happening has not happened, and may never happen. Is God unfaithful? Or, have I set up a formula with stringent expectations? The carnal deal is: 'I wait for twenty-five years and You are obligated to act when I anticipate You acting.' I could get depressed and say, 'Forget it, God.' Or, I can quote the Lord, 'My thoughts are not your thoughts.' I can focus my heart on Him. I can abide in Him and enjoy my relationship with Him, knowing who I am in Him. As Paul said, 'unknown yet known.' Clyde McDowell, my good buddy is now dead. Dying of a brain tumor soon after becoming President of Denver Seminary was not part of Clyde's plan. Before dying he wrote a pamphlet, *The Unexpected Journey*. Clyde did not expect this. Along with Clyde, I must show myself faithful, not believe I am running in vain, and not grow weary and lose heart. What matters is my fellowship with Christ who indwells me, and understand and enjoy who I am in Him." I still recall the moment Clyde called me to tell me of the tumor and to ask for prayer. Sarah and I prayed for Clyde's earthly healing, but the Lord in His wisdom directed the steps of Clyde to a heavenly healing. All of us must allow for the unexpected journey.

This teaching about me being in Christ and Christ being in me helped me in the face of what appeared to be delays if not denials to my prayer requests. This served me to continue to ask for Him to reveal His unique will even though years passed in the face of apparent silence about His unique will on many fronts. I don't mean to downplay God's unique will, but at one level, it didn't matter once I knew who I was in Christ and what God felt about me. I had confidence that He was listening and caring though I heard nothing from Him.

Some folks stop trusting and following the Lord because they interpret the long periods of silence to mean that God doesn't care or have the power to orchestrate their lives. They draw negative conclusions about the character of God based on their seasons of silence. They shut down on the four wills instead of finding pleasure from knowing they are pleasing Him even if He does not respond to them as they hoped.

In reading the first half of the subtitle of this book, which is "The Way He Directs Our Steps," we must keep in mind two things: One, God's timing usually differs from our own. Two, He may direct us in unforeseen ways, as my friend Clyde addressed in his pamphlet, *The Unexpected Journey*.

You in Christ

When you prayed that prayer at the end of the previous chapter, or prayed it as a six-year-old child, something took place in God's eternal judicial system. He redeemed you, accepted you, forgave you, justified you, reconciled you, perfected you, and more. In His eyes an image formed that is endlessly good and immutable. You are His beloved forever and ever, world without end. Unless the Bible taught this, none would dare declare this.

Thus, on this journey of faith, His image of you must become your image of yourself. Though it is a process that deepens over time, you must continue to gain inklings of your true identity before God. You must believe you are who God says you are.

This is crucial since you have rights of access, which directly impact the way you approach God in prayer as you ask for His unique will to be revealed. Said another way, if you lack confidence in God's love for you and doubt that He is for you, you will pull back from praying for His unique will, and will not believe He desires to lead and use you.

Let me share a story that shows how God feels about us. My friend B.J. Weber had a wonderful encounter that evidences that we have worth to God, and God intends for us to spot this (Matthew 10:29–31). B.J. writes, "As I opened the door one day last fall, a disheveled young man, staring at me with glassy eyes, asked 'Are you B.J. Weber?' Clearly distressed, out-of-sorts, and desperate, the young guy fell into my arms and said, 'A rugby guy said I could find help from you.'

"As a graduate of a prestigious university, [we'll call him "Henry"] and after securing a huge job in New York City, Henry was dealing with the first awareness in his young life that he needed help. Drugs and alcohol dominated his youth, and now after resources became more plentiful, he had gone off the proverbial rails. Recovering from a weekend binge, he called a mutual friend who suggested we meet.

"Henry was nervously fingering a penny he found on my front stoop as we sat outside on a beautiful day. He blurted out, 'I am just no good. I have ruined my life, my career, my friendships, embarrassed my family, and now I am living with such guilt that the only thing I can think of is getting drunk again or taking my life . . . I just blew it all.' We moved inside our home and he began to weep uncontrollably. In between sobs and rubbing the penny, he went on. 'I am as worthless as this penny—it's worth nothing . . . like me.' Dropping the penny to the floor, I noticed it was a "wheat" penny, an old penny that the government stopped making in the 1960s. I picked it up and to my amazing surprise the penny was not just an old penny, but a 1909 S-VDB! (In my childhood, I would inspect and sort pennies and coins for my coin collection hobby, and over the years I never found a 1909 S-VDB. Yes, Google it!)

"Rather astounded, I explained to Henry that the value of that seemingly worthless penny, which is indeed a rare coin, is worth much more than he would even imagine. A joyful disbelief filled our hearts and we began to laugh together. Henry told me that it was the first time he had laughed in months. As he looked carefully at the coin, a coin that I had spent my childhood trying to find, he blurted out with a wide grin, 'Do you suppose that this is a sign from God—meant for me to have hope? This is the first day I can say that.' Tenderly, Henry leaned over to me and said, 'You believe in me, don't you, B.J.? No one was betting on me and you, a perfect stranger, helped me.'

"I told him this is like a living parable: What you thought was worthless, in fact, has tremendous value. As our time continued, I reminded him that God does not have 'throwaways.' 'You have tremendous value to God,' I said. 'You are loved with a fierce and powerful love, a love that has eternal hope, a love that is radical and purposeful, a love so amazing that you are reminded of that love by a penny you thought was worthless!'"

God is seeking to get this message through to each of us.

My Awakening!

Let me share my story—soon after my conversion—about why this became so important to me to figure out.

In the first couple years of my faith in Jesus Christ, the following information totally changed my thinking about how God felt about me, which directly affected how I felt about God. His positive view of me changed my view of Him. Perhaps I should have known and valued who He was from the beginning days of my faith, but with most new believers, there is a tendency to interpret how God feels about us based on things going well or bad. It is so easy to conclude "God is against me because I am having all these problems" or "God is for me because everything I want, I am getting." But I needed an illumination about who I was in the eyes of God apart from my painful or joyful experiences.

One of the first struggles I had as a new believer in Jesus Christ revolved around my self-image. Seeing my shortcomings and unworthiness, it was easy for me to conclude that God saw me as I saw myself. Because I saw my unrighteousness, surely God viewed me as unrighteous. Because I had moments where I did not like myself because of my faults, it had to be reasonable to conclude that God didn't like me either. How could He? It seemed like common sense to believe God disfavored me more than favored me. The things I did wrong seemed to weigh more heavily against me than the good I did weighed in my favor. There were moments when these negative thoughts flooded me. I felt unworthy before God. I was not pleased with my thought life, how I reacted to certain people, and my lack of spiritual maturity and passion. I remember thinking that God should reach down from heaven and slap me on the back of the head for my serious imperfections.

Added to this was my experience during the early days while attending Wheaton College, a Christian institution. Entering this Christian culture with some of the brightest and best among conservative Christians, I had to face myself head-on. I had only been a believer in Jesus for a little over two years, and I had no idea that other Christ-followers could be so mature and talented. When I stepped on campus, the first three people I met stunned me with their gifts and genius. I met an All-American football player who looked like Atlas, a concert pianist who played in nationally recognized venues, and a national merit scholar who had his own radio program. Within minutes I felt flooded with the feelings that I was in the wrong place; I was inadequate and a nobody. This put me in a place where many of us find ourselves when we ask, "Do I even matter compared to others who are smarter and better than me?" Added to this was my guilt and shame over the things inside of me that I knew weren't good, like my sinful arrogance, anger, anxiety, and appetites.

Little did I know what was about to enter my understanding of God and myself. During the first several weeks of my freshman year, I met the chaplain at Wheaton College, Evan Welsh. He was one of the most remarkable and loving men I had ever met. While on a freshman retreat, which Dr. Welsh attended, I found out he still did one hundred push-ups a day and he was in his mid-sixties. In front of a half dozen students I said to him, "Dr. Welsh, you are better than me in everything. . . . You do more push-ups than me . . . you are better looking . . . you are more godly . . . you love people more than me . . ." When Chaplain Welsh heard me say he loves people more than me, tears came to his eyes and he grabbed my shoulders while these students watched. He looked straight into my eyes with a compassion I had never felt from another person and he sternly said, "Don't you ever say I love people more than you. You will love people far more than I will ever love them."

I had never been deluged by such concern and love. It so overwhelmed and bolted me that I found myself ready to cry, and feared that I would cry. I had never encountered anything that hit my soul so quickly and deeply. No one had ever spoken to me this way. Not knowing how to respond, I turned around and walked away. I knew that wasn't right, but what I had just experienced left me in shock and awe.

I tell this story because it happened while I was struggling with what God felt about me, and what I felt about myself. Would I be left in the shadows as a nobody compared to all the students who excelled at everything? Did I have value? Surely God intended to use the gifted. He would powerfully lead them. They would be His vessels fit for the Master's use, while I sank to the bottom. To make it worse, I did not like my sinful nature. The good I wanted to do, I didn't do. The bad I wanted to avoid, I ended up doing (Romans 7:19).

Was I fooling myself about wanting to feel special to God? Though I came to Christ in dramatic fashion, was it going to prove nothing more than an act? I knew that God knew the real me, and compared to others He really had little choice other than to set me aside while honoring others as His prized and gifted instruments. I did not want to feel this way but how else could I interpret God's feelings about me?

There were times I'd awaken in the middle of the night wondering about how God felt about me. One such time as I lay there—and this is what profoundly changed me—it was as though God Himself spoke gently to my heart, "If Evan Welsh, a mere man, could love you that much at that retreat, would I love you less?"

That question stunned me. I felt the full weight of this penetrating truth shoot through my body. Something lodged itself deep in my soul. Immediately I said to myself, "Of course You love me more than Evan Welsh loved me. You are God. Evan is a mere man. You love me far more, light-years more, infinitely more, and will never stop loving me!"

Even today I get teary-eyed over that moment.

That realization set in motion a new awareness of how God viewed me. This prompted me to look at what Scripture said was God's view of me. As I got into those Scriptures—some of which I share below—I began to appreciate that I mattered to Him, and I would never stop mattering to Him. He loved me and would never stop loving me.

All of this profoundly affected the way I understood God's desire and intention to work personally in my life. It helped me understand how to look at God in prayer and how He looked at me when I was praying. It aided me in looking at myself the way God looks at me and feeling about myself the way God feels about me. It started a whole new way of thinking.

For instance, I came across this biblical idea that I was righteous in God's eyes. I learned that when I placed my faith in Christ, I was placed "in Christ." It is as though I was totally enveloped in Him so that when God looked at me He saw only Christ. Isaiah metaphorically portrayed this reality. "He has wrapped me with a robe of righteousness" (Isaiah 61:10). Paul addresses this very idea in Philippians 3:9 where he writes, "found **in Him**, not having a righteousness of my own derived from the Law, but that which is through faith in Christ, the righteousness which comes from God on the basis of faith" (emphasis added). Paul captures this truth for the Corinthians. "He made Him who knew no sin to be sin on our behalf, so that we might become the righteousness of God **in Him**" (2 Corinthians 5:21, emphasis added).

How could this be? How could I be righteous in God's eyes when I was unrighteous in practice? I learned of a concept called our position in Christ, or our identity in Christ. That meant that in a legal or judicial sense God made me perfectly righteous. Even though I was guilty, God stamped "Not Guilty" on my forehead. Even though I was unrighteous, God stamped on me, "Righteous in Christ."

When Jesus ascended to heaven as the perfect, righteous One, the Father embraced, accepted, and glorified Him forever. Because I was "in Christ," I went along for the ride, not as a trick as in the Trojan Horse imagery but as a full recipient of the same status of Jesus.

Let me say to you, in this life you derive personal significance from your positions. It might be your position in the eyes of the company, your position in the eyes of your spouse and family, or your position in the eyes of the world. But these positions are not to be the primary source of your identity since all of these are temporary, and if they change, who are you then? For this reason, as a believer in Jesus Christ, your most important position is your position in Christ. Who you are in the eyes of the Father is who you are!

I want you to catch a glimpse of this. Otherwise when life gets tough and bad things happen to you, you could conclude that God is against you, not for you. You could feel that God condemns you and is not listening to you. You could stop asking for God to direct your steps because you have deduced it is pointless. You pull back from God because you have an image of Him as punitive or indifferent. You feel He has an image of you as deplorable. You cease asking Him to work uniquely in your life. You even stop following the four wills of God.

For this reason, let the following truths humble you and change your thinking about God and yourself:

You Have Been Redeemed

Colossians 1:14: "In whom we have redemption, the forgiveness of sins."

Redemption means purchased. We have been bought for a price, which is the blood of Christ. In order to buy us, God allowed Jesus, His Son, to be expended on the cross. In effect, we are worth Jesus to the Father.

You Have Been Accepted

Romans 15:7: "Christ . . . accepted us to the glory of God."

One of the great needs of the human soul is to be accepted, and our Lord accepts us forever! This is an acceptance based on what He has done, not what we have done. This is an acceptance of our deepest spirit that will one day be set free from sin and death. He does not accept our sin but accepts us in spite of our sin. Because of this, we find our hearts longing to please Him, no longer thinking we must appease Him. When we apprehend the Lord's acceptance of us, we feel a freedom to keep moving forward.

You Have Been Forgiven

> Colossians 2:13–14: "Having forgiven us all our transgressions, having canceled out the certificate of debt consisting of decrees against us, which was hostile to us; and He has taken it out of the way, having nailed it to the cross."

We had a debt that we could not pay, but Christ paid our debt on the cross. That caused all of our transgressions to be forgiven, including our future transgressions. Now, when we seek forgiveness, we are actually appropriating the forgiveness that is already ours. Having said this, we can grieve the Lord by our sin. Like any family relationship, we must apologize and express sorrow to reestablish friendship. However, we do not do this to get back into the family. We are already in the family. We seek forgiveness for our daily sins to reestablish fellowship, not to be saved again. This is for communion, not to prevent condemnation. As Romans 8:1 states, "There is now no condemnation for those who are in Christ Jesus."

You Have Been Justified

> Romans 5:1: "Therefore, having been justified by faith, we have peace with God through our Lord Jesus Christ."

In simplest terms, justified means that in the eyes of God it is just as though we have never sinned. To live a life of self-justification is pointless. We cannot justify ourselves, nor should we try. It is better to confess all the wrongdoing since we have already been justified. Ironically, those who know they are justified, stop the excuses for their sin and take steps to correct it. Though God disciplines us for the wrong, He does not do so to get us to jump through hoops so He can declare us righteous. We have already been declared righteous. He disciplines us in order to help us experience the abundant life He has planned for us (John 10:10).

You Have Been Reconciled

> 2 Corinthians 5:18: "Now all these things are from God, who reconciled us to Himself through Christ and gave us the ministry of reconciliation."

Our sin alienated us from God. Consequently, God had just reason to accuse and condemn us for our offenses against Him. But because of Jesus, the Mediator, God in effect said to us, "I no longer have enmity against you. Because of the sacrifice My Son made, He has made everything perfect between us. Our relationship has been made perfect. All is reconciled in My eternal ledger."

You Have Been Made Perfect

> Hebrews 10:14: "For by one offering He has perfected for all time those who are sanctified."

When Jesus Christ offered to die in our place and pay the debt for our sins, all of our imperfections were forgiven in the eyes of the Father. Jesus Christ compensated for all of our imperfections, and when He did, it left us perfect for all time. We are not perfect in experience but in God's eyes in a judicial sense. He declares us perfect by Christ's offering. It is not possible for us to be made more perfect than we already are through Jesus or perfected for a longer period of time! Perfected for "all time"!

You Have Been Made Righteous

> Philippians 3:9: "Not having a righteousness of my own derived from the Law, but that which is through faith in Christ, the righteousness which comes from God on the basis of faith."

In heaven, an exchange was made. All of our unrighteousness was placed on Christ and all of His righteousness was placed on us. We refer to this as the imputed righteousness of God. Now, when God looks at us, He sees the righteousness of Christ. In a practical sense, day after day we are to become what we already are: righteous. Though we are unrighteous in experience, and feel the guilt of our wrongdoing, God has documented us in His ledger as perfected, redeemed, justified, and righteous. There is nothing that can cause Him to stamp "Unacceptable" on those who have been made righteous through Jesus.

You Have Been Given Access

> Ephesians 2:18: "For through Him we both have our access in one Spirit to the Father."

Applying this to myself, Jesus brings me to the Father and says, "Father, this is Emerson. Emerson, this is the Father. Go ahead, Emerson. Share anything you want with My Father." He does the same with you, now and forevermore. We will have access to the Father throughout eternity. This truth needs to hit us like a ton of bricks. We have access to God and will never be excluded. This is why we must trust that the Father is always listening to our petition for Him to uniquely direct our steps; and if He does not lead us as we have prayed, nonetheless we must trust He is listening most attentively. He is not ignoring us. He is countermanding our request for His greater eternal purpose. Father knows best.

You Have Been Born Again

> 1 Peter 1:23: "For you have been born again not of seed which is perishable but imperishable."

Has the thought ever occurred to you that once we are born again, meaning a spiritual birth after a physical birth, we cannot be unborn? Furthermore, after this birth, there is no spiritual infanticide. Nor is there a spiritual abortion at the point of conception. We are always alive and always a child of God.

You Have Been Adopted

> Ephesians 1:5: "He predestined us to adoption as sons through Jesus Christ to Himself."

Another metaphor to describe our relationship with God, beyond being born again, is adoption. Once adopted, we will not be un-adopted. Legally, it is a done deal. Our adoption papers have been signed, sealed, and delivered. There is no reversing the adoption proceedings. We are in the family of God—forever. Our destiny has been set, and we have all the rights of the true Son of God.

You Are Sons of God

> Galatians 3:26: "For you are all sons of God through faith in Christ Jesus."

As Jesus is the Son of God, God considers all of us sons of His as well. This should boggle our minds. We have the status of sonship in the eyes of God. Having been born again and adopted into God's kingdom, we are sons of God in a positional sense as Jesus is the Son of God. Though we do not possess divinity, nor have a redemptive role, and He alone is the only begotten of the Father, stunningly we have been granted certain divine privileges because of our status as adopted sons and daughters.

You Are Heirs

> Galatians 4:7: "Therefore you are no longer a slave, but a son; and if a son, then an heir through God."

Everything Jesus inherits, we inherit. We are co-heirs with Christ. Romans 8:17 states, "and if children, heirs also, heirs of God and fellow heirs with Christ." In our present condition there is no way we can begin to imagine what we are entitled to receive. We are beneficiaries of all that Christ receives. None of us would dare make this claim apart from the Bible revealing it.

This is why, as we follow the four wills of God and we do not experience His unique leading, we can live in anticipation that One Day that will all change, and change it will!

You Have a Heavenly Citizenship

Philippians 3:20: "For our citizenship is in heaven."

We are not alien immigrants hoping to cross the heavenly border undetected. And, we will not be exported when entering the gates of heaven. Instead, we will hear the stamping of our passport and then "Welcome home, heavenly citizen. Right this way. Let me show you your mansion. It's unlike anything you could ever imagine. Jesus had gone ahead to prepare a place for you. Because you were faithful in little things on earth, adhering to the four wills among many other commands, Jesus will put you in authority over ten cities in heaven (Luke 19:17). Your heavenly citizenship entails delightful privileges and fulfilling duties. Ready?"

Will you appropriate these positional truths about you?

Many who set in motion God's unique leading are confident in asking because of what it means to be in Christ. They know they are special to Him not because of anything special they have done but because He is special. He has chosen to love them. Humbly they embrace the fact that He loves them because He loves them. Thus, they come before Him in confident prayer as His beloved, called and chosen (Jude 1:1; 2 Thessalonians 2:13; Colossians 3:12). Their position in Christ justifies this, not their performance. This is all about the performance of Christ on their behalf that enables their eternal acceptance. They are never presumptuous in their petition, only grateful that He always listens out of love, even if after "thrice" praying and nothing happens.

An Analogy

Even if God does not unfold His unique will to you, you can find pleasure in who you are in Christ. You can find joy in your new identity as you go about the mundane stuff of life. By way of analogy, suppose you wondered as a twenty-five-year-old if you should move to Dallas, Texas, start a café, pursue an MBA, and buy a higher-end condo? What would you feel when, during this time of decision-making, you learned that you are an heir to a French king from the 1600s and are to receive $100 million thirty years from now, at age fifty-five? In the meantime, you must fulfill four conditions: learn French, move to France for the rest of your life, manage a cleaning service for thirty years, and tell no one who you are no matter how you are treated. Would you act based on your secret identity, forgo your other plans, move to France, learn French, begin the cleaning service, and rejoice in who you are for thirty years in your undistinguished condition?

Based on the Bible, God's identification of us causes the French heir's story to pale as a bag of peanuts pales to a million tons of gold. We are "fellow heirs with Christ" (Roman 8:17), and though "unknown yet well-known" (2 Corinthians 6:9).

This prompts the question, will you find a measure of pleasure in the assertions God makes about you as an heir, and that one day all of this will be a reality? C. S. Lewis mentions what a schoolboy feels the day before summer break. The anticipation of tomorrow is as real as tomorrow. Living in the anticipation of summer vacation is as exciting as the day the bell rings and we run out the door into the summer breeze for the next three months. In learning how He views you, will your self-image turn positive and will your self-worth skyrocket even though you go about serving in mundane ways among irritable people, as you await for the final bell to ring?

What about Sin?

"Okay, Emerson, but what if we have sinned horribly, surely God doesn't like us at some level?" To this point, a husband committed adultery and bemoaned, "I have hoped to die and died to hope." But in learning of this teaching on his position in Christ, he changed his thoughts and feelings. "I am trusting God's Word about being a new creature with new hope according to my identity in Christ. I choose to walk the balance of my years in integrity with my head high knowing that I am forgiven by a gracious and merciful God of my wrongdoing. Further, I have come to forgive myself . . . regardless of the sins of the past. I know there will be complications and consequences, as there have already been in recent years, but I trust God to enable me to face them by faith in His power." He then quotes Isaiah 43:18–19, "Do not call to mind the former things, or ponder things of the past. Behold, I will do something new . . ."

I agree. God will not ignore our sin. There are consequences. But even God's discipline is rooted in His love to put us back on the right track, not slap us for getting off track. His discipline is rooted in His eternal covenant with us. To Him we are beloved sons of God, co-heirs with Christ. Though it may feel inappropriate to appropriate this teaching, we must lift our heads up high with humble hearts as we face our sin and future. This adulterous husband who changed course and believed in his new identity in Christ put himself in a position to uniquely experience God's love and leading in the midst of God's discipline and ruptured relationships.

What about when another sins against us? One wife wrote to me, "The first week of hearing this teaching on our position in Christ, I struggled not to cry, for I had, for a long time, wondered, *Who am I?* I saw myself only as a reflection of who my husband thought I was, and that was based on performance alone. He is a controller, and for years I have felt less than fully appreciated. I could never do enough, say enough, or respect enough. Failure was my destiny. I felt I had no identity; but you helped me seek the Holy Spirit's power. I asked, begged really, and He answered. It has made all the difference, that God loves me, and He likes me a lot!"

After a sermon series I did on our position in Christ, a person in my church sent to me their new prayer. May I invite you to pray this prayer too, and mean it?

> Hi, Father! It has been a long time since I talked to You. Once again, shame has kept me from You . . . It is so nice to be in Your warm embrace again after so long a time. But now that I know You value me and because I am priceless to You and because You have forgiven my sins and I am worth as much to You as Jesus is and because I am sinless because Your blood has cleansed me from *all* unrighteousness, I come before Your throne with complete confidence. Now that I know my identity and that being "in You" I need not be ashamed to come before Your throne, it is exciting and freeing! . . . I am a new

creation in Jesus, because He has purchased me for an inesti-
mable price and in His redemptive salvation He has washed
me and given me a brand-new life. I woke up this morning
and wondered if I would have to worry about being abandoned and suddenly realized what You said, "I will never leave
you or abandon you." It was a most wonderful and secure feeling to know that I didn't have to worry about that anymore.

By the way, as you echo this prayer, doing so from your heart, you are
acting on two of the four wills. You are believing in Jesus Christ and all that
He did for you and you are giving thanks to God for your eternal position in
Christ. In so doing, you are pleasing God as you keep these commandments.
Let yourself be pleased in pleasing Him.

But there is another major revelation that is equally exciting: Christ in
you.

Christ in You

After people received Christ in my pastor's study at the church, I would
ask them, "Where is Jesus Christ in relationship to you right now?" They
would look at me—some with tears in their eyes and with a sense of wonder
and peace—and say, "He's in me." Then I would ask, "Will He leave you or
forsake you?" They would then say, "No." I would agree, "If anyone was a
perfect gentleman, Jesus Christ was and is that perfect gentleman. And if He
said He'd come into you, which He just did, then He won't leave or lose you"
(John 6:39). Many teared up more. I would then say, "However, let me ask if
in several days, you do not feel His presence, has He exited?" They would get
it and answer, "No." I explained that for this reason we must not let feelings
dictate our faith but let our faith govern our feelings.

When you received Christ, the Spirit of Christ took up residence within
you. You became the temple of God. To every Jew in the first century this
was a revolutionary teaching. The Jews were clueless that the Messiah by His
Spirit would indwell the individual. When Paul talks about a "mystery," he
means God revealed a truth to the Christ-followers that the Jews would not
have known or predicted. What was one such mystery? We read in Colossians
1:27 that "this mystery . . . is Christ in you." The Jews had been taught that

when the Messiah came, He would literally dwell in the physical temple in Jerusalem. Now, those who had received Christ learn that *they* are the temple of Christ.

> Galatians 2:20: "I have been crucified with Christ; and it is no longer I who live, but Christ lives in me; and the life which I now live in the flesh I live by faith in the Son of God, who loved me and gave Himself up for me."

> Ephesians 3:17: "So that Christ may dwell in your hearts through faith."

> Romans 8:9: "However, you are not in the flesh but in the Spirit, if indeed the Spirit of God dwells in you. But if anyone does not have the Spirit of Christ, he does not belong to Him."

> 1 Corinthians 3:16: "Do you not know that you are a temple of God and that the Spirit of God dwells in you?"

> 2 Corinthians 6:16: "For we are the temple of the living God."

If you have received Christ into your life, then the Spirit of God, or the synonymous expression "the Spirit of Christ," has taken up permanent residence inside of you. So what all does this mean?

What Is Positive about Christ in You?

Did you know that God could live anywhere, but He chose your heart? He is present in you.

The motif of this book is that when we act on the four universal wills of God, we encounter God's unique moving in our lives. Part of God's unique moving for each believer is to experience His presence.

Brother Lawrence, a monk known for his ability to *"practice the presence of God,"* testifies to experiencing God's love for him while washing dishes. Indeed, he claims that he felt a greater sense of God's presence when doing practical tasks than when he was in worship services. Though we don't see any miracles, something happens that fills us with awe and wonder in God Himself. It may be that while we are meditating on Scripture, praying, worshipping, or working we feel God's peaceful presence descending on our soul.

A godly woman lived in the 1700s and by our standard of living she would be considered very poor. But listen to her words:

> *I do not know when I have had happier times in my soul* than when I have been sitting at work, with nothing before me but a dim candle and the white cloth I am sewing, and hearing no sound but that of my own breath, with God in my soul and heaven in my eye. I rejoice in being exactly what I am, a creature capable of loving God, and who, as long as God lives, must be happy. I get up and look for a while out of the window, and gaze at the moon and stars, the work of an Almighty hand. I think of the grandeur of the universe, and then sit down, and think myself one of the happiest beings in it.[1]

As this woman conveys, we can be happy in abiding in Christ as we know He abides in our soul.

Years ago several families in the church I pastored traveled with my family to Mississippi where we ministered to a poverty-stricken location. While there I had the privilege of visiting with an aged African-American woman who loved Christ. Over her lifetime, she worked in the cotton fields. As we sat on her front porch, I asked her to share her upbringing. "How did you survive all those years laboring in the scorching hot cotton fields?" She told me, "Each morning I'd awaken before dawn. The day before me would be another day of drudgery in the cotton fields. To make it through the heat and humidity, I'd ask the Lord to give me a song for the day. If I had a song, I could hum and sing it while picking cotton. Faithfully, He'd give me a song. Each day I'd sing to Him and *find comfort in His presence.*"

How does one begin the experience of God's presence? Ask God to show you how. A person emails about what to do during hardships. "I think the best advice I have for a person in a difficult situation is to make a firm decision not to stay handcuffed to any circumstance that allows resentment, bitterness, unforgiveness, and anger to take root in the heart. Those emotions can surface constantly, but if a person makes it their goal to invite Jesus to go everywhere with them, and to determine to grow and mature, instead of wanting comfort, the Lord will bring about the change in them necessary to be joyful and happy in that difficult situation. You have to train for godliness, just like you train and prepare for everything else in your life. *Tell the Lord you want the revelation of Christ in you, and He will reveal all that He is.* Of course, this is a process. For me it has taken three to four years to really make this exchange a reality, but I live in a very free place in my life. Also, a choice to serve others in some type of ministry really takes the focus off of you and puts it back on Christ. This really works, but you have to choose maturity over comfort and keep the truth pouring into your heart, so that your faith becomes more of a reality than your emotions and circumstance. You know, we all want spiritual growth, but we don't want the experiences that bring about that growth!"

I hope your heart is stirred with experiencing more of God's presence in your life, but there is a way to resist His presence.

What Is Negative about Christ in You?

You can distance yourself from Him. You can refuse fellowship with Christ.

Jesus makes this point to the church—believers in Him—when He says in Revelation 3:19–20, "Those whom I love, I reprove and discipline; therefore be zealous and repent. Behold, I stand at the door and knock; if anyone hears My voice and opens the door, I will come in to him and will dine with him, and he with Me."

Though Jesus still resided within them, they refused communion with Him.

Years ago I married a godly couple, he with a genetic defect that confined him to a wheelchair, she with horrible scars all over her body from burns that had also left her maimed. Nonetheless, Mark and Kim envisioned a wonderful life together, one that would include having children. They consulted specialists who assured them they could have a healthy child. They prayed and prayed for God's guidance. Finally, feeling the advice from genetics experts was part of His leading, they went ahead and had a baby girl, Elizabeth—who was born with the same genetic defects as her father. Shock turned to deep disillusionment. Mark and Kim both felt bushwhacked by God. They asked the inevitable question: "Why?" When He did not answer, they pulled back from God and away from each other. Their anger and disenchantment grew, and even though our elders prayed with them, their home remained full of negative tension, and their hearts remained cold toward God.

Two years later Kim came to my office to tell me about something extraordinary that had happened. Although numb toward God, she had continued having a devotional time. A Christian friend had encouraged her to keep reading the Bible, and because she respected this friend so much, she did so even though she didn't feel like it. One morning during her devotional time, Kim sensed Christ's presence on the other side of the room. Then she felt an inaudible voice: "Kim, are you ready to open your heart to Me?"

"No!" she said firmly, and the Presence was gone. Christ had stood at the door of Kim's heart and knocked, and she did not invite Him in for sweet communion that she enjoyed in the past. But she could not remain hardened after her encounter, and she had come to me, her pastor, for help. We prayed and Kim opened the door of her heart, saying, "Lord, not my will, but Your will be done." His presence filled her soul, and we rejoiced together. Not long after Kim regained fellowship with God, Mark turned the corner as well, yet to this day their heavenly Father has been silent about the "Why?" And, their daughter, Elizabeth, who grew to be a godly and wise young adult woman, recently died.

When God allows difficulties to come your way that leave you hurting and confused, what do you feel about God? The prophet Jonah got angry when the Lord did not operate according to his expectations. Jonah entered such an angry state that he requested to die (Jonah 4:).

You too can get mad at God. You can feel He failed you. Though Christ indwells you, you stop praying, reading the Bible, and worshipping. You distance yourself. Though Jesus gently knocks at the door of your heart to reestablish communion with you in the face of your unanswered questions, do you do what Kim did? Do you refuse to open the door? Do you protrude your lower spiritual lip in an immature pout, as though this kind of negativity will motivate God to apologize, make things right, and do your will?

Won't Leave, Won't Lead

At these moments of madness, He won't leave you but neither will He lead you.

In Ephesians 4:30 we read that a believer can "grieve the Holy Spirit of God" and in 1 Thessalonians 5:19 can "quench the Spirit." In other words, you can sadden Him over something you have done and block Him from doing what He would have done. You can quench Him like someone quenches a fire. You suppress and stifle the intended purpose of God in your daily life.

This does not mean God is thin-skinned or weak. That caricature is erroneous, but your unholiness affects Him. As His adopted, inheriting child, you matter to Him, and He is susceptible to your unrighteous anger and carnal choices. Your unholy heart affects the very holy heart of God. By way of contrast, the Greeks opposed this idea of God being affected by humans. They declared that God was indifferent to human beings since a god affected by people would put humans in the upper hand, above the god. But our God is not less than God when grieved and quenched. In His wisdom and sovereignty, He adjusts until we confess our sin and change our ways.

God continues to shepherd us and knocks at our door to reestablish communion with Him, like He did with Kim. In His wisdom He has plan B, C, D, and an infinite number of options. By way of an analogy, which we have uniquely in the twenty-first century, is the GPS instrument. As we head in a sinful direction, which grieves and quenches Him, He comes to us at a certain point and softly knocks on our heart. "Will you stop your stubborn resistance and let Me redirect you?" He not only directs our steps, as the subtitle of this book declares, but He re-directs our steps! We've all heard GPS announce, "Recalculating!" Our loving, wise, and powerful God recalculates. Yes, His re-direction may entail His discipline, but it is not punitive for getting off track; it is His way of helping us back on track. His discipline is designed to help us be more self-disciplined.

One day it hit me, "This is not about me begging God to show up in my life but about me not grieving and quenching His presence in me." He has already shown up. Christ is in me. I am His temple. I may not feel Him but He is in me. By faith, I can have the confidence that He is unfolding His unique purposes.

"But Emerson, what if I don't know if I am grieving and quenching Him?" I would say don't worry about it. Paul wrote about himself in 1 Corinthians 4:4, "For I am conscious of nothing against myself." Believe God is actively working in, through, and around you. As John said in 1 John 3:21, "Beloved, if our heart does not condemn us, we have confidence before God."

"But Emerson, what if I do know that I grieved and quenched Him?" If you know this, quickly confess, "Lord, I am so sorry for what I said and did. I know I grieved You. Lord, forgive me for quenching Your moving on my behalf. Please help me change in this area. I reopen my heart to You. In humility, I make myself available to You for Your purposes. Your will be done. In Jesus' Name." The apostle John also penned in 1 John 1:9, "If we confess our sins, He is faithful and righteous to forgive us our sins and to cleanse us from all unrighteousness."

Whatever God's unique will may be for your life, one thing is certain: He will be with you as it is carried out. If you have chosen to believe in Jesus Christ, one of God's four universal wills for your life, then the Spirit of God is already there, ready to go! And, if you are in a dark patch that has stretched out for years without much direction from God, like someone confined in a prison cell, He is still with you. Be confident. Be cleansed. You may not be experiencing God's unique will for you as you had hoped but you can experience Christ Himself. Enjoy Him! Abide in Him as He abides in you.

Chapter 5
GOD'S WILL: GIVE THANKS IN EVERYTHING

The universal will of God in 1 Thessalonians 5:18 says, "In everything give thanks; for this is God's will for you in Christ Jesus."

Paul said these words hundreds of years ago; but if he hadn't, my wife would have. Sarah's life embodies this verse, and she lived it while having cancer and a double mastectomy. The discipline of praise so powers her perspective that she decorated our kitchen wall with giant wooden letters declaring: "IN ALL THINGS GIVE THANKS." Imagine meeting that reminder at the coffeepot each morning and at the end of long days! Giving thanks is sometimes tough enough, but "in everything"?

Yes, in everything. God calls us to give thanks for the good things and the "unseen good things," momentarily disguised as bad things. While doing the latter may sound impossible and unreasonable, which we will address, let's begin by asking if we neglect giving thanks for the things that are obviously good.

Permit me to ask you this question: In the past, after God uniquely led you, did you give thanks for His wonderful leading? Do you recall turning your heart toward the Lord and praying, "Lord, thank You for Your kindness in directing my steps"? In the presence of other believers, did you say,

"Would you join me in giving thanks to the Lord for His personal intervention on my behalf?"

We need to consider if the Lord does not direct our steps as we hope because He takes note that we do not thank Him when He has in the past. Though none of us will give thanks perfectly, we can be less imperfect.

Give Thanks for the Good Things

Consider the ten lepers that Jesus healed when He entered a village on His way between Samaria and Galilee. Luke 17 records the story this way: "Ten leprous men who stood at a distance met Him; and they raised their voices, saying, 'Jesus, Master, have mercy on us!' When He saw them, He said to them, 'Go and show yourselves to the priests.' And as they were going, they were cleansed" (vv. 12–14). All ten were cleansed!

Here is the interesting part: "Now one of them, when he saw that he had been healed, turned back, glorifying God with a loud voice, and he fell on his face at His feet, giving thanks to Him. And he was a Samaritan" (vv. 15–16).

Is your response to this story the same as Jesus' response? Jesus said, "Were there not ten cleansed? But the nine—where are they?" (v. 17). Jesus healed all of them, but only one returned to give thanks. Imagine that! Though miraculously cleansed of disease and delivered from social disgrace, nine of them dart off without yelling back, "Hey, Jesus, thanks!" Even more astonishing is the fact that the grateful one was a Samaritan, a sect of Jews who were looked down on by the religious elite.

Are we any different? How often do we give thanks for the good things in our lives? Despite an economic downturn, most of us will still enjoy one of the most comfortable lifestyles in human history. We have friends, employment, health, recreation, and a myriad of material goods such as houses, cars, televisions, and the list goes on. Did I say the list goes on? Yet, do we regularly give thanks to God? Or, do we feel we deserve what we have and only fixate on what we don't have? The apostle Paul laments the ingratitude of believers: "For even though they knew God, they did not . . . give thanks" (Romans 1:21).

When we give thanks for what we do have, acting on 1 Thessalonians 5:18, we not only obey God, we also see life and people more positively. God begins to give us glimpses of good things that He is weaving into our lives. James tells us, "Every good . . . and every perfect gift is from above, coming down from the Father of lights" (James 1:17). Giving thanks opens our hearts to receive these gifts. One wife, who had been married forty years, wrote me that one night she felt God saying to her: "I want you to imagine you are a giant highlighter, and I want you to highlight all those things that are honorable and true about your husband. See your husband through My eyes."

She got up and started writing, filling pages with why she respected her husband and was thankful for him. She rejoiced when, "God filled me with His love for my husband and shone His light into our relationship." In obeying God's universal will about giving thanks, she encountered the love of God in her heart. She was then able to see God's goodness in things that she had previously overlooked or took for granted.

Giving thanks triggers powerful insights and even the love of God. Jude tells us "keep yourselves in the love of God" (Jude 21). Maybe this is one way of doing this.

Give Thanks for the Unseen Good

Since God intends, as James says, to give us "good and perfect gifts," do you find it peculiar that we don't give thanks for the good in our lives? If you find that odd, you will find this odder. God also calls us to give thanks during the not-so-good times. My friend Sam Ericsson, a man with a Harvard Law degree who founded Advocates International, lived a life of thanksgiving. He calls 1 Thessalonians 5:18, Paul's "Golden Rule for Losing." Before his death, Sam left many of us with an example of someone who gave thanks continually, no matter what. Sam comments:

> "In *everything* give thanks for this is *the will* of God in Christ Jesus," means we party when we win, and we party when we lose. I can't recall when this hit me, but I realized that 1 Thessalonians 5:18 is not there for just the wins. Obviously, we all party the births, promotions, and weddings. But 5:18 is there for cancer, death, and terminations. As I like to say, "There is good news and there is other news."

You can't tell whether the "other news" is good or bad until *all* the facts are in. The example I use is that of the first Good Friday, when the Romans crucified Jesus. Can you imagine saying to Peter Friday evening, "Hey, Peter isn't this a *Good* Friday?" He would have looked at you with disdain. It wasn't until Sunday morning three days later that The Event began to sink in for the disciples. After the Resurrection, it indeed was Good Friday, not Bad Friday. Thus, everything to Sam was Party Time.

Sam recounted one powerful example from his own experience. He says, "I had bladder cancer, but I was in remission. However, July 18, 2003, when I fell and broke seven ribs, puncturing my right lung, the doctors discovered that the bladder cancer had spread to the left lung, something I would not have discovered until it was too late! Thank God for 'the fall' down the steps."

Sam chose to give thanks because of the clear message in the Bible to give thanks. Anybody read the Psalms lately? Even when David is crying out in utter agony, he usually begins or ends the psalm with praise. Sam mirrored this spirit. He literally threw scores of parties on the heels of defeat because he believed God was up to something good during each setback. That's why Sam always signed his letters, "Living in His-Story." Sam modeled the idea of giving thanks for the good and the unseen good. In his faith, every bad Friday would prove to be a Good Friday.

Give Thanks in the Moment of Crisis

Are there events so horrifying that giving thanks seems foolish or impossible? Consider this scenario. Some friends told me of an extraordinary worship service in Uganda among Ugandan Christians. Though they had been living in the midst of real evil and suffering, including genocide, the worship leader requested everyone to, "give thanks to God for all that we have." The group then participated in the kind of spirited worship African believers are known for and which can shame many of us. They were dancing about and thanking God for all that they had, which by our standards fell below the poverty line! Then the leader caught the American group off guard. "Okay, now let's really worship and thank God for what we do not have." The Ugandans escalated their thanksgiving and praise. My friends were stunned at the deep spirituality. Yes, God is honored when we fill the moment of our need with the power of praise to Him.

When Paul instructs, "In everything give thanks," he means in everything—in plenty or poverty. Such thanksgiving should arise independent of circumstances. Though good things should prompt our gratitude, the absence of good should trigger our praise as well. Painful circumstances must not fool us into concluding that only bad will come from the situation. If we lose the hope that God is working all things together for good, we have lost faith in our Sovereign God (1 Timothy 6:15). We must trust that our Bad Friday possesses an unseen good so wonderful that we will soon refer to it as our Good Friday. The cross leads to the crown. A thankful heart declares to God, "I believe all things are working together for good" (Romans 8:28).

I need to make a clarifying point here. When I give thanks, I never thank God for the evil per se, but that He intends to work all things (which includes the evil) together for good. If not on Earth, it will surely be true in heaven. But this distinction is important to make so we don't grow confused as though we are to be happy about wickedness.

How do we give thanks in the midst of horrendous circumstances and loathsome people? Joseph, in the Bible, toward his wicked acting brothers who years earlier sold him into the slavery that took him to Egypt, captures the correct interpretation. Because of a famine in Israel, his brothers sought help in Egypt. However, they soon discovered Joseph was not dead, but governed as second in command to Pharaoh. Fearing his revenge, they instead heard Joseph say, "As for you, you meant evil against me, but God meant it for good in order to bring about this present result, to preserve many people alive" (Genesis 50:20). Every believer can imitate Joseph's faith perspective without endorsing vile activities.

Give Thanks for False Alarms

Are you like me? I am great at petitioning God for what I need; but sometimes when I no longer have that need, like the nine healed lepers, I don't even think about God, and certainly don't thank Him for helping me with the need!

But I do something else that is equally unfortunate. I ask God for help only to realize later I have sounded a false alarm. For example, recently, our bank account showed we had only twelve cents. Since last year the media reported the increase of electronic theft, I thought, *Has someone stolen money from our account?* Concluding that we had been victimized, I prayed, "Please God, let there not be an electronic thief; and if so, may we recover our money." After praying, I tried to discover what had happened. When I learned that we had two accounts, one of which had been sitting dormant with twelve cents, I felt tremendous relief and went on my way.

An hour later, I remembered my prayer for help and observed that I had never thought about thanking God about the false alarm. I hadn't even given Him a second thought. I reasoned that since no hacker had broken into my account and stolen all my money, thanksgiving was, therefore, unnecessary. Why thank God when I was the one who had sounded a false alarm? How shameful! I should have at least prayed, "Father, thank You that I had no crisis. Thank You that it was a false alarm. Thank You for a banking system that has a fail-safe system in place." I could have come up with a half-dozen reasons for thanking Him, but instead I went on my merry way like one of the nine lepers. I was good to go.

This episode got me to thinking about God's promise in Isaiah 65:24, "It will come to pass that before they call, I will answer." How many times did God intervene before I prayed because He fore-heard my prayer? Jesus said, "Your Father knows what you need before you ask Him" (Matthew 6:8). Because we can't see the future, we don't know how to pray accordingly. As an act of mercy, He goes before us and protects us from what He sees and we don't. Wow. Perhaps that is why Jesus taught us to pray, "Lead us not into temptation." As I repeat these words, they make me wonder how many times God has protected me from temptation without me knowing it. Yet, did I ever thank Him? No. Because I didn't see what He had done, I went on with no thought of thanks for God's protection. For all the times He "leads me not into temptation," He deserves my thanks. The problem is that I don't see this, so I must give thanks by faith! We walk by faith, not by sight.

Some of us do not give thanks unless we see a miracle. We reduce every good event to a natural cause and rationalize that God had nothing to do with it. We marvel at the coincidence, but we do not worship. After things work out, we conclude, "Oh, it would have worked out anyway," and we go on our way. However, if things do not work out, we get angry at God for not helping us. When violent, destructive forces like earthquakes, lightning, and tsunamis occur, we refer to them as "acts of God." But when good things happen, we call it "luck." God gets little thanks and much blame.

We often lack the same perspective when it comes to marriage and family relationships. We let the list of things we "don't have" overwhelm the things we do have. Many parents, children, and spouses recount only the things they feel they are missing in these important relationships. Because of this tendency to fixate on what the others don't provide them, they miss the good that is already there. When challenged to write down and give God thanks for all the positive things they do have, they often divulge that they have let their hurts sound a false alarm. One wife wrote, "Every day I am writing one thing I am thankful for about my husband, and then most days sharing it with him as an encouragement. I want to set my mind on my husband's good points . . ." What can you thank God for right now?

- *Give thanks for the many good things you possess.*
- *Give thanks for the difficult things that God will bring to good.*
- *Give thanks for the fact that things could be worse if false alarms prove true.*
- *Give Him thanks for preventing the bad things you never saw.*

No, really, go ahead and give thanks. Stop reading and give thanks.

I believe that the people who act on this universal will of God find their obedience triggering the unique responses of God to their lives. It is the kind of obedience that delights God.

The Miracle of Giving Thanks

One of the most impressive examples I can remember of the importance of giving God thanks was recounted by Merlin Carothers in his book *Prison to Praise*. Though I read it years ago, I have not forgotten the story of Ron and Sue in chapter 8. In fact, I called him personally to confirm the story, which he did.

While Ron was serving in the Army during the Vietnam War, he found himself in near despair. It was not because he had received orders to head straight to Vietnam, but because his wife Sue had attempted suicide when he'd received his draft papers. She was now threatening to end her life if he went to the battlefront. Her childhood memories of being abandoned made her terrified of being once again left alone. Having been put up for adoption by her biological family and then having her adopted family sever all ties with her later in life, Sue feared that Paul would die and that she would once again be without a family. Death seemed a better option than loneliness.

When she met with Merlin, who was a chaplain in the Army at the time, Sue heard him say, "What I want you to do is to kneel here with me and thank God that Ron is going to Vietnam." He pointed out to her Paul's words in 1 Thessalonians 5:18, "in everything give thanks; for this is God's will for you in Christ Jesus." In near hysterics, she exited his office crying. When Ron met with Merlin the next day to clarify his counsel, he heard the same message: "I want you to kneel down and thank God that you're going to Vietnam and that Sue is so upset that she is threatening to kill herself." In disbelief, he left.[1]

Both Ron and Sue claimed to be believers in Jesus Christ. However, neither had focused attention on this text or applied it in this manner. At a crossroads, Ron and Sue had to decide: Would they act on this Scripture? Would they believe, as Merlin pointed out, that God was working all things together for good (Romans 8:28)? Would they try to thank God for what they were encountering? Concluding they had nothing to lose, they returned to Merlin. With great struggle and heaviness of heart, they knelt and prayed as best as they could. After leaving his office, they went into a chapel and began thanking God for the challenge before them.

Ron had duties to fulfill so he left the chapel, but Sue returned to the chaplain's office. As she sat in the waiting room, a soldier entered and wanted to see the chaplain. As the two began to chat, Sue found out that the soldier's wife was divorcing him. After hearing his woes, she told him that it would do little good to hear this chaplain's advice. The soldier continued to pour out his heart to her instead and eventually pulled out his billfold to show her pictures of his wife, children, and other family members. When he flipped to one photograph, Sue screamed, "That is my mother!" He replied that it could not be: "I don't have a sister."

Sue explained her adoption to him and then confessed that as a child she had rummaged through her parents' desk and landed upon a photograph of her real mother. According to Sue, that photograph and his photo were of the same woman.

Sue was correct! She was talking to her flesh-and-blood brother! Then the realization came crashing home. She was not alone in this world. She had a brother and a family. God had heard her prayer of thanksgiving.

What were the statistical odds of that very brother walking in minutes after Sue thanked God for her worst nightmare? Who could guess? But, God clearly wanted to give Sue a sign of His loving-kindness. Through this episode, He spoke into her heart a profound truth: "I am your heavenly Father, and I can move heaven and earth to bring you a family. Trust Me, Sue. Give Me thanks. Don't despair to the point of suicide. Never conclude you are without family."

Many others, like Sue, have thanked God while still in the midst of crisis and then lived to see a dramatic change of circumstances. Do you remember what happened to Jonah when he cried out to God from the belly of the whale? If you know the story, you know the whale coughed him up on dry ground. But, do you remember what the turning point was in his destiny? Jonah says: "While I was fainting away, I remembered the LORD, and my prayer came to You, into Your holy temple" (Jonah 2:7). Note the key point here that follows: Jonah does not just cry out to the Lord, he gives God thanks. His next words are:

"I will sacrifice to You with the voice of thanksgiving" (v. 9). And then and only then, does the Lord command the fish to vomit "Jonah up onto the dry land" (v. 10).

Giving thanks makes things happen.

Will you give thanks to God at this moment in the midst of your issue? I believe you can encounter something beyond your wildest imagination.

A Sacrifice of Thanksgiving

I cannot promise that you will undergo a "chills up the spine" episode like Jonah or Sue did, but you will sense God's blessing. The distressing events may not change quickly, but your heart will change as you honor God with your praises. When we offer God thanks for His goodness in the midst of our pain, God calls this a "sacrifice of thanksgiving." One of my wife's favorite

verses is Psalm 50:23: "He who offers a sacrifice of thanksgiving honors Me."
Sarah's journal records this note:

> I remember when our son, David, had broken his leg quite
> severely while playing baseball in the eighth grade. As I saw
> his heart breaking over the loss of a dream to play in the major
> leagues someday, I realized I could not fix his leg or his dream.
> Now my heart was breaking also. How would I get through
> this? Then God showed me this wasn't a crisis with my son,
> but a crisis of faith for me. I knew it was God's will that I
> give thanks in all things, but this didn't feel like something
> for which to be thankful. And that is when I learned about a
> "sacrifice of thanksgiving" in Psalm 50:23. A sacrifice is just
> that, a sacrifice. Since then I have chosen to give thanks when
> I don't see the good.

What exactly is a sacrifice of thanksgiving? Quite simply it involves giving up something of value. The Old Testament records two types of sacrifices
to Yahweh: sacrifices for the atonement of sin, and sacrifices as an expression
of praise and worship. The sacrifice of thanksgiving is an example of the
second type. To this altar, the worshippers brought the firstfruits of their
crops as well as tithes and incense. The sacrifice of atonement, by contrast,
involved blood: meat and burnt offerings for trespasses and sins. While the
non-blood sacrifices were an expression of praise and the blood sacrifices
were offered to atone sins, notice, however, in the verses below that the spirit
of thanksgiving supersedes the literal sacrifice in both:

> Psalm 50:13–14: "Shall I eat the flesh of bulls or drink the
> blood of male goats? Offer to God a sacrifice of thanksgiving."

> Psalm 69:30–31: "I will praise the name of God with song
> and magnify Him with thanksgiving. And it will please the
> LORD better than an ox or a young bull with horns and hoofs."

The goal, therefore, of both types of sacrifices is praise. Whether the
thing sacrificed is grain or the blood of bulls, the spirit of worship is what
God desires. In the New Testament, therefore, the sacrifice of thanksgiving

is heard in the praises of the early church for the sacrificial death of Jesus. Today, as we offer thanks for the seen and unseen good in our lives, we continue this practice of offering a sacrifice of thanksgiving.

When Sarah offered a sacrifice of praise for our son's situation, she surrendered to God her will, emotions, and right to understand the situation. Years later when Sarah learned she had breast cancer, she was so disciplined in this practice of offering thanks that she immediately offered up a sacrifice of thanksgiving to God. Though she did not always feel like giving thanks, she chose to place her life on God's altar for Him to use as He saw fit. She had no human knowledge that things would work out well, but her sacrifice of thanksgiving let the Lord know that she trusted Him *in* the situation and *with* the situation.

The giant wooden letters in our kitchen, "IN EVERYTHING GIVE THANKS," expressed her goal then. They now remind us of God's goodness through it all.

Chapter 6
GIVE THANKS IN EVERYTHING, REALLY?

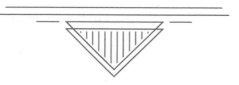

"In everything, give thanks." Everything, really? Are there no exceptions?

Several years ago while we were presenting the message of the four wills of God at a conference, we met a couple who had no idea that in a few hours they would be asked to apply the message of thanks in all things. Shortly after the talk, they received news that their son was dead. Though he had been driving the speed limit, he rounded a corner and collided with a tractor combine taking up both sides of the highway on a bridge. He had no options: he could not stop or go off to a side of the road.

In the middle of the night, the words of 1 Thessalonians 5:18 came to this couple. They sensed the Lord saying, "I want you to give Me thanks. Not for the death of your son, but for how I intend to use your son's death." They obeyed by giving thanks, but they admitted that it felt like a true sacrifice since they knew they would never see their son again. They continued to give thanks even as they struggled to live with the unanswered question: "Why, God, did You allow our son to die? Why?"

Though this couple testifies to the overwhelming things God has done around the death of their son, they still endure dark nights when they go to God's altar with nothing to offer but a sacrifice of praise for the lost son whose smile they will not see again.

Christ's Example in Suffering

Humanly, it makes little sense to give thanks to God for His goodness when bad things are happening. Ultimately we must believe as Jesus believed, and we must behave as Jesus behaved: Christ becomes our model. As Matthew tells us, "And when He had taken a cup and given thanks, He gave it to them, saying, 'Drink from it, all of you; for this is My blood of the covenant, which is poured out for many for forgiveness of sins. . . .' After singing a hymn, they went out to the Mount of Olives" (Matthew 26:27–30). Jesus gave thanks even though evil would soon engulf Him. He sang a hymn even though Roman centurions would soon place Him on a wooden cross and whack nails through His hands and feet. Even at this dire moment, Jesus trusted in the Father's goodness and gave thanks.

And do not miss the key point here: It was Jesus' ability to give thanks to God while suffering at the hands of evil men that released Him to accomplish the greatest work of all—God's forgiveness of men. Jesus offered up a sacrifice of praise and, in so doing, purchased our redemption. Indeed, giving thanks may be the ultimate expression of the redemptive love that leads to forgiveness.

When It Seems Foolish to Give Thanks

What are some of the hardest times for you to offer a sacrifice of thanksgiving? When does it seem ridiculous or nearly impossible? Think for a moment of things in your life that you have struggled to understand and accept, and you will likely hover close to the kind of hurts that wound us all—loss, betrayal, abuse, injustice, lack of opportunity, or the fulfillment of basic needs. The hurts of some, however, exceed understanding.

A woman in my church wrote to me of her sufferings. Not only did her father and grandfather abuse her, later her dad killed his girlfriend and then killed himself. On top of this, her mother struggled with alcoholism, and one day slit her wrists in front of her. Soon the courts assigned her to a foster care family in which the parents who took her to church on Sunday would molest her on Sunday afternoon.

In response to my counsel concerning the giving of thanks, which I felt so unworthy to present to her in light of her sufferings, she wrote: "As you pointed out, it's easy to stand in total faith when God is doing what you want in your life. The true test comes when His plan differs from yours. I prayed God would change my circumstances. Because I did not see an answer to my prayers, I stopped praying. Now I can humbly see that even a Spirit-filled believer can become the person you described: One who questions God's love and turns away in disobedience. I was that person and that decision to turn away from God led to the most painful experiences in my life for many years. I see now that the Lord was working things together for good even when I didn't feel it." Trusting in God's goodness, she asked Him back into her life though her questions about evil remain unanswered.

In giving thanks, evil must not be minimized. But in refusing to offer a sacrifice of praise, the only recourse is to push God out of one's life for allowing the evil. This woman did what most do who refuse to trust God and give thanks in spite of the evil. To insure "justice," she judged God as unloving, which in the end achieved nothing for her.

Can You Give Thanks and Still Ask "Why?"

Does offering a sacrifice of praise answer the question "Why, God, did this happen?" Not likely. But, is it wrong to ask, "Why?" Absolutely not! Jesus Himself asked "why" while He hung on the cross. In His agony, He cried out, "My God, My God, why have You forsaken Me?" (Matthew 27:46). Though there are things we will never understand until God answers them in heaven, He promises to meet us in our pain as we offer our praise (1 Corinthians 13:12).

For many, the most difficult part of offering a sacrifice of praise is the burden of doing it day after day, month after month, year after year without anything to mitigate the pain. While God often provides grace and comfort in the midst of crisis, some hurts never change or, at least, seem to take forever to change. How, for instance, do you keep giving thanks for the weighty complexities of being disabled or being the caretaker of one who is? How do you remain thankful for years of difficulty due to an accident, loss of employment, or the betrayal of a spouse or friend? How do you stay thankful for a difficult marriage or the ongoing hurts of a prodigal child? How do you rejoice over years of infertility, or the long wait of some singles to find good spouses?

It is not easy! Hannah, who eventually bore the great prophet Samuel, spent years of weeping before the Lord as she prayed for a son. Because she kept her face toward God in her time of suffering, she was able to offer God her song of praise when He fulfilled her heart's desire (1 Samuel 2:1–10). Some, like Hannah, begin in faith and thankfulness and yet grow weary over time. Does God leave them? No. Even Elijah, after praising God for his victory over the prophets of Baal, collapsed in the wilderness and cried out for death. Before he was again able to seek God, God gave him a chance to rest and eat "angel food."

Make no mistake: Offering up a sacrifice of praise is a choice, and it may feel like "work." But, the good news is that God meets us in our sorrow just as He met Hannah in her tears and Elijah in the wilderness.

Sarah, my wife, says, "I encourage everyone going through a time of suffering or confusion to offer God a sacrifice of thanksgiving." She loves to offer this sacrifice even if she sees nothing happening. After her cancer and double mastectomy, she waited for years not knowing if the cancer would return with a vengeance. Her sacrifice—a form of praise and worship— releases her faith. It provides her with confidence that God is working even if she cannot see it.

Give Thanks When God Allows Suffering and Evil?

Some do not think it wise or logical to offer praise to God for trying events. One pastor shared with me about the death of his four-year-old daughter. Bewildered by her death, he and his wife asked the fundamental question: "Is God good?" They concluded, "Yes," and offered a sacrifice of thanksgiving, even though God never revealed to them why He allowed their precious daughter to die.

Later, they shared their conclusion about God's goodness with the congregation. Several couples left the church. These couples had fervently prayed for the healing of the four-year-old; but with her death, their faith floundered. They concluded that because God did not respond to their worthy prayer, then He lacked love or power. Because they had believed God had power to heal her, they concluded God must be unloving if He did not heal her. When this pastor declared his firm faith in God's goodness, they felt confused and betrayed. Though they had been taught the biblical idea of the mystery of suffering, when unexplained suffering knocked at their door, they chose to walk away from faith rather than embrace God's unseen goodness in and through it.

Believers who resent and reject God like this will not experience His unique leading. One cannot shake a fist at God in bitterness and refuse to trust and thank Him, as if spiritual pouting could force God's hand to provide an explanation to "Why?"

Indeed, the issue that causes more people to turn from God than anything else is the apparent contradiction that a loving God could allow so much suffering, especially when that suffering stems from evil intent.

One woman in my church shared with me her story of ritualistic abuse. As a child, her parents engaged in satanic worship. The things to which they subjected her cannot be printed here. Years later, as a young adult not knowing how to make sense of her childhood, she came to see me. She said, "When I first saw you, I was saying to God, 'WHY? Why, when you could see what was happening, would you not want to protect a little child?'"

Overwhelmed by her story, I admitted that I had no answer. But, in obedience to Scripture, I tenderly asked her, "Have you thanked God for what happened? I say that because I have found that thanksgiving serves as a means of grace in dealing with evil, as odd as that may seem." Not surprisingly, she sat there in utter disbelief and anger. However, she later told me:

> I couldn't believe you would tell me to give thanks for my horrible situation! Even so, your words haunted me because I desired to obey God. I moved forward in faith because you told me I could start by asking God to help me to *want* to be thankful. I started by telling God that if this was what He wanted me to do, then I needed Him to help me to want to be thankful. I asked Him to help me know how to tell Him I was thankful. I refused to say, "Hooray, God, thanks for all the bad things that happened to me; that was some good time." Over time, God helped me understand that I could be thankful because of how He brought me through and for the

person He was going to help me become. After that, I gave thanks. Today I stand back totally amazed at how God protected me from physical, emotional, and spiritual death. I also see how my past could have shaped me one way, but giving thanks shaped me another.

Thank God in the Face of Evil?

This woman's victory over the evils that oppressed her youth was released by giving thanks. But, let's not minimize evil! Neither let us deny the goodness of God in the face of evil. Corrie Ten Boom, who suffered at the hands of the Nazis, shared:

> Often I have heard people say, "How good God is! We prayed that it would not rain for our church picnic, and look at the lovely weather!" Yes, God is good when He sends good weather. But God was also good when He allowed my sister, Betsie, to starve to death before my eyes in a German concentration camp. I remember one occasion when I was very discouraged there. Everything around us was dark, and there was darkness in my heart. I remember telling Betsie that I thought God had forgotten us. "No, Corrie," said Betsie, "He has not forgotten us. Remember His Word: 'For as the heavens are high above the earth, so great is His steadfast love toward those who fear Him.'"[1]

Betsie's death might well have left Corrie embittered toward God; but instead Corrie concludes, "There is an ocean of God's love available—there is plenty for everyone. May God grant you never to doubt that victorious love—whatever the circumstances."[2]

Over the years as a pastor in a college town, people asked how an all-loving and all-powerful God could allow evil to triumph. But that isn't just a question for intellectuals. Everyone asks this question. For me, I remember coming to a point when I read the Gospels, the narrative of the life of Christ, that I would trust Christ based on what I knew about Him in the face of my unanswered questions. I chose that posture as opposed to distrusting Christ based on what I knew about Him in the face of my unanswered questions. See the difference? No matter what, there will be unanswered questions about evil. Yet, Jesus Himself, who endured evil beyond anything we can imagine, trusted in Abba Father's compassion and authority. Jesus asked "Why?" but continued to trust in God the Father in the face of His unanswered question. I absorbed the truth that Jesus intends for me to imitate Him. The reality of evil brings each of us to this crossroads. Will we choose to give thanks to God in the face of our unanswered question about suffering and evil because we trust what we know about Him?

A Thankful Heart Forgives

Forgiving, as hard as it is, is not an option for the believer: Jesus prayed, "Forgive us our debts, as we also have forgiven our debtors" (Matthew 6:12). John makes it clear that forgiveness is evidence of God's work in us. In 1 John 4:19–21, he says: "We love, because He first loved us. If someone says, 'I love God,' and hates his brother, he is a liar; for the one who does not love his brother whom he has seen, cannot love God whom he has not seen. And this commandment we have from Him, that the one who loves God should love his brother also."

One of the surest ways, therefore, to miss experiencing God's will and blessing for your life is to refuse to forgive. Yes, there are hurts that wrack the soul and losses that can never be replaced. Yes, there are injustices that beg for retribution, perhaps even punishment. But, the deeper the pain and the more heinous the evil inflicted, the more obvious it is that nothing can be done to replace the loss. Forgiving is the only means of releasing the offender and freeing the spirit of the injured. How does this process begin? In the same way it did for the women who were victims of child abuse and the couples who lost a child: by first giving thanks.

Some contend that the hardest part of giving thanks and forgiving occurs when new offenses continue to occur. Though they may have found strength to endure the big crisis, the onslaught of repeated injuries exhausts the soul. Whether it is a demeaning boss, a harsh spouse, a rebellious child, or losses due to illness, they struggle to rest in God's peace because the consequences must be born every day. Giving thanks and forgiving must be a daily discipline in order to survive. One single mom I know explains it this way: "Forgiving my husband for the way he treated me during the divorce and custody process was just the beginning. For many years after, he verbally abused me and said things to try to turn the kids against me. When I thought things couldn't get worse, he married a mutual friend and moved nearby. Crazy as it seemed at the time, I followed the counsel of friends and determined to ask God for the grace to forgive the both of us for the choices that had brought us to this point.

"Yes, this felt like a foolish thing to do! But, as I gave thanks, God let me see His love in rescuing me from a highly destructive situation. Though I had prayed for our marriage to be healed, when all doors closed, I began to see that God would bring His good in a different way. And He did! More blessings than I can count.

"The best part may have been watching my kids get a head start in seeing how God's forgiveness is worked out in real time. As we walked it through together, we became bonded in God's love, and we learned that forgiving is an ongoing process, something that is utterly impossible to do apart from God's grace."

This single mother's ability to give thanks in the midst of ongoing pain allowed her to lead her children to rest in God's father-love. She told me, "Without God's grace we never could have begun to forgive. But, without giving God thanks—even while in the middle of the mess—we would not have felt His grace. Giving thanks was the turning point to a new life for me and my children."

A thankful heart stays at the foot of the cross, aware of its own need for forgiveness and the need to forgive others. Just as we can never right our wrongdoings to please God, some wrongs done to us or by us cannot be righted, repaid, or replaced. The debt is too large. As this young single mother learned, giving thanks releases the debt and opens the heart to a new life. It lets you enjoy what you already have, gives you hope that God is working through the "unseen good," and reminds you that there are ways you are being protected that you don't catch.

So I wonder: If thanksgiving is so powerful, why isn't it our first instinct? Why don't we do it before we can see a good reason for giving thanks?

Do Only Fools Thank God Ahead of Time?

Cal Rychener, the pastor of Northwoods Church in Peoria, Illinois, shared with me a great story about how he learned to give thanks. He said, "I remember a situation from 1979. I was home for Christmas from college; and one afternoon, when just my mom and dad and I were home for lunch, as I approached the table I saw my dad with his head down in his arms. That was very unlike him, and I said, 'Dad, what's the matter?' He said, 'I've got a $300 fuel bill that I don't know how I'm going to pay.' Everything inside of me wanted to say, 'Dad, let's pray about it, turn it over to God, and see what He does about it.' But I didn't say that. I didn't want to sound super-spiritual. I didn't want to get my hopes up that God might do something and then see nothing happen. That's the real tension in faith. If you truly believe God for everything, there are going to be times that you'll feel like an idiot for trusting Him because until He comes through you don't know if He's going to. If He doesn't, then you feel like maybe you weren't supposed to trust His promise like that. So we play it safe, and worry and fret instead of trust!"

What Cal decided to do in this situation was pray. He says:

> I went up to my bedroom after lunch because I was feeling bad for my dad, and I got down on my knees and prayed for him. "Lord, Dad just never has had anything to spare with all of us kids. It's always been so hard for him. Please bless him and provide for this fuel bill somehow." I will never forget his coming up the walk that day at 5:00 p.m. with a surprise Christmas bonus that the boss had given to all the employees that day. Care to guess the amount of the bonus? Three hundred dollars! What a great answer to prayer!
>
> But I remember praying, "Lord, I want to learn how to cultivate a heart of faith and joy at noon before I actually see You solve the problem at 5:00." The circumstances said at noon, "You're in a heap of trouble. You're not going to be able to pay your bills. You've got a reason to feel hopeless and dejected," and from our natural surroundings, we did! But, those were the lies that were designed to take my eyes off my Source! I was not any less secure at noon than at 5:00 p.m.

Because of this, I want to trust God and give thanks to God ahead of time. I want to learn to pray, "Thank You, Lord. Though this fuel bill is due; and I don't know how I'm going to pay it, You are the Source."

Cal then shared that he is still learning to activate his faith through thanksgiving: "For me, the secret to operating in faith is found in this little word—thanksgiving."

God Responds to Our Sacrifice of Thanksgiving

Years later, as the senior pastor of Northwoods Church, Cal and his church board had the opportunity to purchase extra land for their exploding church. The price? Three hundred thousand dollars. They didn't have $300,000, so they discussed borrowing and other options. Having learned over the years that thanksgiving releases his faith, Cal offered to God a sacrifice of thanksgiving. Knowing that he only wanted what God desired for the church, he did not worry. His thanksgiving lifted his burdens and brought peace and confidence. The next day a businessman in the church sent Cal a check for $300,000. This man had no idea about the need or the board discussions. He simply felt led by God to give the church a check for $300,000.

Cal doesn't receive miraculous interventions like this every time he prays; but these experiences have taught him that giving thanks allows him to remain calm and anticipate God's goodness regardless of the outcome.

What is your need? Are you thanking God ahead of time? Are you learning to relax and release your faith through the giving of thanks?

Sadly, many of us never learn this. When the $300 bill comes at noon, we pound the kitchen table in anger or kick the wall. Like Job's wife, we want to "curse God and die!" The miracle at 5:00 p.m. never comes because we've released ourselves to anger not praise. The Bible says, "The foolishness of man ruins his way, and his heart rages against the Lord" (Proverbs 19:3).

Friend, don't ruin your way in this adventure of experiencing the unique will of God. Don't clench your fist in frustration. Open your hands to heaven and give thanks. Yes, it's a sacrifice—a sacrifice of praise—but God receives your offering!

Hebrews 13:15 suggests, "Through Him then, let us continually offer up a sacrifice of praise to God, that is, the fruit of lips that give thanks to His name." If we reject this instruction, our hearts will be too hard to hear Him speak His unique leading for us. His silence won't be because He wants to keep us at a distance, but because we have closed our hearts to Him. If, however, we give thanks for the good and the "unseen good" in our difficult times, God will reveal His unique plans for us.

Chapter 7
GOD'S WILL: SUBMIT IN DOING RIGHT

Will We Submit in Doing Right When No One Watches?

I have a married friend who told me that his wife lost a $2,800 diamond. Fortunately, his insurance policy covered lost jewelry. When he reported the lost diamond to his agent, he was informed that the company would immediately cut a check for $2,800. The only caveat was if the lost item was later found, they required that the owner either return the money or hand in the lost item. My friend understood the terms. He and his wife took the money and purchased a new diamond. As it would happen, a couple years later, they found the lost diamond down the crevice of a suitcase. My friend's immediate thought was, *No one needs to know and now we have a diamond we could sell for $2,800.* However, his next thought came from the Lord. *You need to submit in doing what is right.* My friend knew 1 Peter 4:19 where Peter tells the believers to "entrust their souls to a faithful Creator in doing what is right." Would he trust God and submit in doing what was right, though he would kiss goodbye the extra $2,800, or would he sell the diamond and pocket the extra money? He called the insurance agent to report that they had found the lost diamond and would be returning the prized jewel to headquarters. He told me that as he hung up an extraordinary peace and freedom flooded his soul. He knew he had done the right thing in submitting to the insurance company's terms. He had a clear conscience and God was pleased.

How many of us would do the opposite of my friend? We reason, "Hey, submitting in doing what is right will prevent me from gaining an extra $2,800, whereas doing what is wrong when no one will know the difference will put a nice chunk of change in my pocket that could be very useful."

I ask this because, when the insurance company's headquarters received the $2,800 diamond in the mail, an administrator reported back to my friend's insurance agent, "We have never had a person send headquarters an item that was lost but then found. We don't know what to do with the diamond. Should we keep it or sell it? We have no policy in place since this has never happened." Even though their contract explicitly tells the insured to do this, no one ever did until my friend!

One would think more would send in the lost item since doing so would relieve the guilty feelings we are certain to have for submitting in doing what is wrong. Ill-gotten gains (Proverbs 10:2) rob a person of sleep and cause one to look over the shoulder. Fear of exposure is enslaving, whereas doing what is right enables one to sleep like a baby. The subconscious never forgets, and neither does the Lord. The believer gets away with nothing, both suffering the loving discipline of God as well as forfeiting the unique leading and favor of God.

At a deeper level, my friend perceived this was a test of his faith and obedience toward God's will. This wasn't an issue about stewardship or shrewdness but about who he would be before God, no matter what.

I can tell you this about my friend: few are encountering the hand of God in their lives like he is. God's favor is all over this gentleman. There is a correlation between the hand of God being upon us and us keeping our hand out of the till.

What Is Submission?

This universal will of God on submission is located in 1 Peter 2:13–15. "Submit yourselves for the Lord's sake to every human institution, whether to a king as the one in authority, or to governors as sent by him for the punishment of evildoers and the praise of those who do right. For such is the will of God that by doing right you may silence the ignorance of foolish men."

When Peter wrote in verse 15, "For such is the will of God" is he referring to what he said just before that about submitting to authority? Or, was this a prelude to what he said immediately after about doing right to silence foolish men?

Both.

First, it related to submission to authority because of the larger context. Peter addresses submission with several groups. We are to submit as citizens (2:13), as slaves (2:18), as wives (3:1), as husbands "in the same way" (3:7), and as the younger (5:5).

Submission literally means to place under or rank under. We submit by placing ourselves under or ranking under another's authority. Such submission is a choice we make. We are the ones who choose to obey the command.

In 1 Peter 2:17–18; 3:2; and 3:7, Peter instructs everyone—particularly slaves, wives, and husbands—to put on honor and respect when submitting in doing what is right. Submission includes both actions of deference and attitudes of deference. When a person submits in action but shows contempt in attitude, that individual misses the spirit of Peter's instruction. Paul teaches the same and specifically states we are not to be "disrespectful" (1 Timothy 6:2).

Why does God command us to respectfully submit? Because we don't have a natural craving to do this on our own. If we did, the command would be moot. It is not natural to be respectfully submissive when required to do what we do not want to do. We prefer not to defer when it demands sacrifice. Something in us wants to be unsubmissive and disrespectful when told to do what we do not want to do. The fact is, most submission entails doing what is legally required according to the rules and regulations of the institution, and those policies are not evil per se, just demanding. We do not submit to an authority who demands we do what is wrong.

Second, this is why Peter stresses "doing right" (1 Peter 2:15), the other dimension of submission. We submit in doing right regardless of an authority figure standing over us.

What does it mean, "doing right"? Paul may help us understand what the apostles meant. We read Paul's instruction in Titus 3:1–2, "Remind them to be subject to rulers, to authorities, to be obedient, to be ready for every good deed, to malign no one, to be peaceable, gentle, showing every consideration for all men." Are we:

- obeying the rules,
- ready to do good deeds,
- maligning no one,
- peaceable,
- gentle, and
- considerate?

If so, we are submitting to doing what is right in the eyes of God.

Authority figures themselves must submit in doing right when no one oversees them. This is the reason the Bible tells them to recognize that they too have a Master (Ephesians 6:9; Colossians 4:1). Ultimately, all of us do this "for the Lord's sake." On a practical note, some of us live independently enough that we are not under the watchful eye of a supervising authority figure (Luke 12:45). Our focus needs to be on submitting in doing what is right for the Lord's sake when we have the freedom to do what is wrong and can get away with it before other people.

Why else submit in doing what is right when no one is looking? If we have critics—and most Christ-followers do—those critics will look for us to do something wrong, or notice it when we do. For this reason, when we keep submitting in doing right, we silence the foolish critics insofar as having hard facts against us. They cannot slander us for doing wrong since we did nothing wrong. Yes, there will be people criticizing us for doing right. People thought my friend an idiot for turning in the $2,800 diamond. There might be mockery, but there can be no incrimination. The mockery and criticism will quickly die without substance. When, though, we submit in doing wrong, and we have critics who find out, they will use this against us to our humiliation and punishment. No one will come alongside of us and praise us.

According to 1 Peter 2:13–15, such submission prevents punishment for wrongdoing and garners praise for doing right, silences the false and foolish critics of our faith and values, and in effect wins the approval and protection of those over us.

As odd as it sounds, when we submit in the way Peter addresses, we exercise spiritual authority over the hearts of those over us! Submission leads to influence. There is power in submission. However, this happens over time, and may not happen at all. The issue is following God's will in submitting in doing what is right regardless of the outcome, but always with the vision that God will favor us (1 Peter 2:19–20).

So then, there are two dimensions to submission: One, submit to what an authority figure rightfully requires of us. Two, submit in doing what is right independent of an authority figure because it is the right thing to do.

For this book's purposes, let's combine those two dimensions to define submission as: respectfully doing what is rightfully required by an authority figure even when we don't want to do it, and doing what is right apart from an authority figure because of our reverence for Christ.

Is Submission Merely an Inconvenience?

Trust me, I've well heard the hesitation and concerns that may be coming to your mind: "Emerson, you need to be cautious on this topic of submission. There are bad authority figures out there and people could misread what you are writing here and go along with bad leadership. We must 'question authority.' Besides, too many authorities are ripping us off and we need to even the score where we can."

The mere mention of the word *submission* ignites fear and anger in some folks, probably from an excruciating encounter with an abusive authority figure. I empathize with their knee-jerk reaction, but we must not indict every authority on the basis of a few bad apples. But this alarm is why not a few say to me, "Of the four wills, the one on submission really troubles me, and it is the one I struggle with the most."

Unfortunately, fearing the worst side of submission, they inadvertently subvert the teaching on submission. In ringing the bell about the dangers or stupidity of submission, they ignore the safety and wisdom of such submission, not to mention contravene the Word of God.

So, let's get on the same page. We should never submit to authority figures who require us to lie, steal, or cheat. Nor should we submit to those who tell us to renounce our faith in Jesus Christ. God never intends this.

But for most of us, that's not our predicament. We are not living inside a totalitarian regime that mandates by absolute decree that we reject Jesus

Christ. In our daily life, no one compels us to be unprincipled and thereby compromise our morality or faith.

Instead, we are addressing when an authority figure requests that we do something that is an inconvenience, not iniquitous. The authority's request may annoy us but doing what they expect hardly turns us into an apostate. We may have to make changes, but none that make us criminal.

For instance, management changes the beginning of the work shift from 9:00 a.m. to 6:00 a.m. There is nothing immoral, illegal, or unethical in this decision. Asking their employees to come to work at 6:00 a.m. may not be the best of decisions by management, but it is not a wicked requirement that demands we submit to evil and sin. Yet, one would think with some folks being asked of this that an evil edict had been delivered and that mutiny, not submission, is God's will. But we all know that coming to work three hours earlier is hardly submission to a heretical lifestyle or grounds for a rebellious coup.

The type of thing that should lead to insurrection is if you were a German citizen in the year 1939 and were commanded to submit to German Nazis who demand that you turn Jews over to be executed. We must not submit to that. It may be "legal" but it isn't moral. Submission here would be qualitatively wrong and wicked.

Gray Areas versus Black-and-White Issues

For this reason, we must always distinguish between comparative issues and qualitative issues. By that I mean, 9:00 a.m. compared to 6:00 a.m. may be a better time to start the workday. Who doesn't want to sleep in? But that is a comparison that can only allow us to argue that one decision is better than the other, not that one is intrinsically evil and the other is intrinsically good. To argue that management has made an evil decision with the 6:00 a.m. start time is to make a qualitative judgment, and that is more wrong as a judgment against management than management's decision to order us to be at work at 6 a.m.

We'd be arguing that qualitatively 6:00 a.m. is an ungodly time and thus unbiblical to start work, whereas 9:00 a.m. is the time God intended people to start work. Of course, that's as laughable as it's untrue. Management's mandate to start at 6:00 a.m. is not vile. This is not a black-and-white issue.

Therefore, if we have a rebellious attitude toward 6:00 a.m., we are not following the will of God. We are not submitting to authority for the Lord's sake in doing what is right according to management.

And, yes, it is right according to what management says is right. This is a gray area that allows for a great deal of legitimate differences of opinion, none of which are wrong—only different. In gray areas, management has the right to make the rules on what is right for the organization. As long as it isn't illegal, immoral, or unethical, we need to yield to the rule.

Just because something doesn't feel right to us doesn't make it morally wrong. Our feelings are often due to being irritated by inconvenience, not due to our faith and conscience being compromised. We want to do what we want to do when we want to do it, and we do not want to do what our authorities want us to do when we do not want to do it.

"But Emerson what if the inconvenience is too much for us since we have to care for an elderly grandmother from 7:00 a.m. to 8:30 a.m., feeding and dressing her?" If we have the freedom to quit this job and work for another company, so be it. Grandma overrides our present employment. We are not defiant for resigning. This is a gray area. We are free to come out from under the company's authority structure based on our priorities and conscience. On the other hand, as long as we work under this company's authoritative hierarchy, God calls us to submit to 6:00 a.m., and to submit without a defiant attitude. As for our grandmother, we will need to figure out a way for someone to care for her from 7:00 to 8:30 a.m. This is our responsibility, not management's.

When Making an Appeal, Be Appealing

Can we respectfully appeal to management to keep the starting time at 9:00 a.m.? Most organizations have lines of authority through which appeals can be made, and if so, the answer is absolutely yes. Or, one might ask for an exception in order to take care of Grandmother. Companies can be accommodating, and even coworkers can support us coming in at 9:00 a.m. while they come in at 6:00 a.m. if they know of our grandmother. Most management and coworkers are not without grace. But during the appeal process, we must say, "I intend to come to work at 6:00 a.m. and do my job as I always have done it. I will follow your decision. However, I wanted to express my concerns and preferences. Thank you for allowing me the opportunity to communicate with you." Most leaders respond positively to people who communicate their opinion with a submissive and respectful demeanor.

Too often, conflicts arise between employees and management because the employee displays a rebellious attitude, and it is to this attitude management reacts. Management isn't reacting to the substance of the concern, but to the employee who launches right in with, "I plan on quitting this job if you have us start at 6:00 a.m. I am sick and tired of management's bad decisions." The employee's contempt and threats become the culprits, not the list of grievances that could have been communicated respectfully and submissively. When we make an appeal, we need to make sure they are saying no to the substance of our petition and not because they are so offended they won't give us the time of day.

The test of our submission comes when the authorities deny our request to keep the time at 9:00 a.m. Will we follow what Peter tells us: "Submit yourselves for the Lord's sake to every human institution"? Will we show deference, knowing we are following God's will and putting ourselves in a favorable position for God to honor our obedience to Him?

Remember: following the universal will of God activates the unique will of God. Though we may not get our way with management, we will know that we have obeyed our Master.

Giving the Authority the Benefit of the Doubt

Though earlier in our lives some of us were horribly treated by a parent, teacher, coach, man, uncle, boss, or pastor, we must not indict the whole based on a particular. Though this negative experience has put a bad taste in our mouths toward authority, we must not let ourselves view all authority as guilty until proven innocent.

As tough as it is, we need to return to the wisdom of the courts: people are assumed innocent until proven guilty. Unless there are facts to prove guilt, we must not allow our past mistreatment to cause us to project onto all future authority figures the label of Abuser.

It is not appropriate to have a defiant spirit toward authority figures as a way of protecting ourselves from being hurt again. Maybe we were too naïve earlier as we blindly trusted, but we do not become wise by impugning a leader's motives and showing contempt when there are no facts that prove the leader is corrupted.

When we justify our rebelliousness as self-protective, we end up making enemies of people who are not our enemies. They may bother and annoy us with their requirements, but they are not out to abuse us.

Are you making the wrong people your enemy? Are you being asked by decent people, albeit imperfect, to respectfully do what is rightfully required of you but you have a chip on your shoulder? Will God unfold His unique will for you if you have clenched fists, ready to strike first?

Bad Authority or Bad Submitter?

Consider this story of two sons in their twenties living at home. Though the sons' parents had established the rule of no drinking or smoking at home, one day the mom arrived home to find her two sons, along with some friends, puffing away in the backyard. Shocked, she reminded the sons of the family rule. Claiming they were adults, they told their mom that they could smoke if they wanted to smoke. When things escalated into a heated fight, the mom, in utter frustration, smashed some dishes. The sons responded by calling the police. When the officers found out the facts, one officer zeroed in on the sons saying,

> Let me get the facts straight. You are living on your parents' property, not working, paying no rent, and eating free food. Furthermore, you have one basic rule: don't smoke or drink on the premise. Because you don't like that rule, you called the police on your own mother. Yes, she smashed dishes, but that's not why you called. You called the police to punish your mother for her rule. What kind of men are you? Get a life. Move out if you don't like the rule.

Some of us need to hear this will on submission precisely because we fool ourselves like these two sons into thinking that those "over" us take advantage of us, when often we control the situation through our resistance and coercion. We claim victimhood but harbor an attitude of entitlement and make controlling demands. Though we perceive ourselves as submitting to the boss, parent, government, spouse, teacher, or board, we display a disposition of disgust. Or, we utter threats such as, "I will sue you," or "I am running away," or "I refuse to pay taxes," or "I won't be treated like a doormat," or "I won't do the assignment," or "I won't follow the board's policy." We claim the authority is bad when we are a bad submitter.

I recently heard of one Christian couple who refused to pay taxes for thirteen years despite the clear counsel of Romans 13:1, 6–7. As native Hawaiians, they felt their heritage entitled them to a God-given exemption. They rationalized their position by convincing themselves that the authorities had no right to enact this tax.

Another man illegally copied DVDs from a ministry. When a group member queried, "Did you get permission to copy these?" he retorted, "No way! They shouldn't sell the Word of God." He believed he had a right to disregard copyright laws because he felt ministries should not charge. Of course, it didn't enter his mind to donate to the ministries!

Some refuse to submit to the loving counsel of church elders. The leadership at one church gently confronted a husband for yelling at his wife in the church parking lot (Hebrews 13:17). After this truthful rebuke, the husband left the church. He claimed he intended to obey God, not man, which warped the meaning of Acts 5:29.

Such stories seem endless.

Will such people experience the unique will of God? Unlikely. Their pet peeves and attitudes sabotage all that God intended to do on their behalf.

Are We Demanding and Coercive?

What can we learn from the two brothers who tried to coerce their mother and the police, the couple in Hawaii who willfully ignored the law to pay taxes, the man who defied copyright laws, or the husband who rejected the church leadership as having no right to confront him?

These people see themselves as right and righteous. However, they have become self-righteous and self-deceived. They are neither teachable nor submissive. They do not see themselves as the problem. Those making the rules are to blame.

The brothers hung onto their "poor me" attitude, believing that they were the victims, not their mother. The couple in Hawaii clung to their belief that they had a legal entitlement to refuse paying taxes. The guy who copied copyrighted material dug his heels in since in his dogmatic opinion he represented God's view. The husband who left the church after the elders confronted him saw himself biblically justified to confront and reject the leadership.

The human heart does not naturally submit nor show respect to those God calls to be authorities over us. The heart is naturally defiant when inconvenienced or not getting what it wants. Sadly, some of us don't see this part of our lives.

What makes this hard to discern about ourselves is when we see ourselves as so caring and conscientious that we blind ourselves to our controlling and contemptuous methods.

Do you recall the story of Martha and Jesus? She complained to Jesus that Mary, her sister, neglected to help her with the preparations to serve the guests. Instead, Mary sat at the feet of Jesus listening to Him. Martha boiled. She bristled as she made preparation for the meal. Then, fed up, Martha engaged the perfect, loving, and caring Son of God and asked a stunning question: "Lord, do You not care that my sister has left me to do all the serving alone?" She then barked a command to the Command-Giver, "Then tell her to help me" (Luke 10:40).

Martha looked into the eyes of Love and told Love itself that He does not care. In effect, she felt that she cared more than the Son of God cares. She then ordered the Lord of lords to do what she requested. She took control by telling God what to do. I have a hunch that Martha requested the apostle John to include this story about her to give testimony to how we can fail to see ourselves at various moments when we feel unfairly treated. We can turn controlling and irreverent and not see it.

Learn It Early or Learn It Late

Recently I counseled a man in his forties who was employed in a huge family-owned company. As a result of the company's success, this man possessed everything the world offers. But, more than anything, he desired God to use him. However, as an adult son working for his father, he struggled with submitting to his dad who exercised final authority in the company. I told him that unless he responded correctly to his father, I didn't believe God would bless him or use him in the way he hoped. Though he agreed with the principle, he struggled to obey it. He knew that if he did not deal with God's instruction, the Lord would not fully bless him with a clear conscience, His divine presence, an effectiveness in prayer, and a fruitfulness in ministry. Because he still harbored adolescent attitudes of disrespect when he felt criticized by his father, he almost tendered his resignation and walked away from the opportunity of his life. At forty, this man still struggled to demonstrate a submissive attitude, something he should have learned as a teen. There are no exceptions: learn it early, or learn it late.

Again, one can be respectful and submissive in demeanor and accomplish the same thing that one feels can only be accomplished via a disrespectful and nonsubmissive demeanor. Knowledge and wisdom carry their own weight. This forty-year-old son didn't need to clench his fists and growl while making his substantive points to his dad.

Granted, not every authority makes requests of us that we deem to be wise and necessary. Peter makes this point absolutely clear in 1 Peter 2:18. Some authority figures make unreasonable demands on us because they are not good nor gentle people. But if it isn't immoral, is the Lord using this to prepare us for His unique mission?

I think of Jesus at age twelve who stunned the religious leaders as He taught them in the temple in Jerusalem. But it was not time for His ministry to begin; and when His parents found Him there, they required of Him to return home. But note what Luke records, "And He went down with them and came to Nazareth, and He continued *in subjection* to them. . . . And Jesus kept increasing in wisdom and stature, and in favor with God and men" (Luke 2:51–52, emphasis added).

When you submit in doing right, it can lead to an increase in wisdom, stature, and favor with God and people. There is an upside to submission. Take heart when the deference is not your preference! In time there can be incredible dividends.

My pastor, Jeff Manion, shared his experience of submission that was a turning point in his encounter with God. He told me, "I was seventeen, the

summer between my junior and senior year in high school. I was an avid run-
ner and training for the Sacramento Marathon. I know a race may not seem
like a big deal, but as a seventeen-year-old, this was HUGE to me. And my
training was well underway. Because I was working in the state of Wyoming
for the summer, I needed my father to get me registered there in Sacramento
where the family resided. During our next phone conversation, my father
told me that he discovered that the marathon was on a Sunday and that he
didn't want me running a race on 'The Lord's Day.' This made a lot of sense
to him, and no sense to me. However, I did something highly uncharacter-
istic. I said, 'OK.' Without a fight and without drama, I simply said, 'OK.'

"Somehow, in that moment, I was conscious of the fact that the Lord
had placed my dad as an authority figure in my life, and that to respond
respectfully to my dad's authority was—not simply to submit to him—but to
submit to the authority of Christ in my life. Something hit me deeply in my
heart that I couldn't respect Christ while disrespecting my dad. In retrospect,
I believe this was a huge breakthrough in my faith journey. It was not only
about obeying my dad, but more to do with submitting to Christ's authority.
My walk with Jesus rocketed forward at this point."

As Jeff reflects today, he knows that if he had argued belligerently about
his right to run on Sunday and been defiant, he would have forfeited a
major breakthrough in his relationship with the Lord. However, because he
obeyed the universal will of God on submission, he activated his experience
of the unique will of God, which he sees clearly now as an adult. Something
changed between Christ and him. Jeff demonstrated to God that he would
submit to His authority and unique leading because he submitted to his dad's
authority and unique leading. There is a correlation.

Have We Learned to Submit?

Most of us are under authority by our choice, and we know that we
could come out from under the authority if we chose. So what do we do
when the authority tells us not to do something and we see it as a good thing
for us to do? Should we leave the authority structure or stay?

I assume that in most cases the authority figure does not have evil will
nor requests us to do evil. Most authority figures try to do what is best for

the organization. The boss may be misguided here and there, but the boss does not have ill will. Even so, we strongly differ with the requirements. So, should we leave or stay?

If we are the compliant type who never steps out in faith, maybe this is the time to change jobs and launch out on something that is new and more compatible with our interests. If we are the defiant type who will eventually lead others, waiting longer could be the advisable route given one has not learned well how to submit.

Whoever we are, have we learned submission in that we know how to consistently and respectfully do what is required of us? If not, it may not be time to exit. God has great plans for us, but if we have not learned to be submissive, then it isn't time to push eject on the job.

B.J. Weber, the former chaplain of the Yankees, and my good friend since the '70s, talked to me about his days of rebellion in Dubuque, Iowa. As the town rowdy in his late teens and early twenties, he ignited trouble in most of the places he frequented. For example, one evening he set the record in the city for the most tickets—an embarrassing number of violations according to B.J. He lived a reckless life to cover up his empty soul. He yearned for meaning but could find no significance. Referring to himself as, "a rebel in search of a cause," he joined SDS (Students for a Democratic Society) and actively participated in the anti-war and hippie movement of the 1960s. Nothing, however, could answer the deep questions in his heart.

Living in Dubuque, a heavily Catholic community with Trappistine nuns and Trappist monks, B.J. visited New Melleray Abbey to purchase the monks' bread. As B.J. walked out of the monastery with a loaf of bread, a monk at the foot of the stairs—Father Mathias—initiated a conversation with B.J. "Hey, you look interesting, what are you all about?" B.J. wanted bread that he purchased for his mother, not a conversation. But he said, "What do you care?" However, the humble, loving Father Mathias didn't let it go. As the conversation continued, Father Mathias invited B.J. to have a cup of coffee. He recognized that B.J.'s hunger for homemade bread paled in comparison to his hunger for the Bread of Life. As the dialogue deepened, the men discussed the purpose of life, and B.J. turned the conversation and asked derisively, "So what are you all about?" Father Mathias replied, "I am about Jesus Christ. And I am here to pray for people and their burdens and I know you are carrying a lot of burdens."

This led to a conversation about how to get to faith. Eventually Father Mathias told B.J., "The first step is to invite Christ into one's life."

Right then it was as though someone lit a match in B.J.'s dark soul. Frightened and exposed, he stayed in the light to feel its warmth and new-found friendship. Could Jesus be the Light of the World, he wondered? Could Jesus be the Bread of Life?

B.J. invited Christ into his heart and something good happened. This began a holy cleansing for B.J. His shame and defilement from darkness and evil behavior lifted. B.J. took his first step to become a Christ-follower.

Living with a gal, he told her what happened. He was so excited, saying, "Something happened with Jesus and God and me, and this monk, and he wants me to come back and study the Bible." Upon hearing that, she moved out the next day.

Sometime later, B.J. moved onto the farm to serve the monks and nuns. Mother Columba, head of the convent, took special interest in this young man who a year later entered a Presbyterian seminary in Dubuque. Like a mother, she counseled him almost on a daily basis in the things of Christ. So, when Sherwood Wert of Billy Graham's *Decision Magazine* heard B.J.'s testimony and invited him to share it at a Billy Graham crusade in Cincinnati, Ohio, B.J. hurried to the convent to inform Mother Columba of this incredible invitation to share Christ with thousands. "What do you think, Mother?" "B.J., you are entirely too young in your faith. This would ruin you. I don't think you should do this." Shocked, B.J. naively replied, "Well, I'm going to do this." "If you do this, we will always love you but you can only visit us on weekends. You cannot stay here." B.J. was stunned and puzzled as to why she would not sanction him responding to the opportunity to share the love of Christ with thousands. He could not believe what his ears were hearing. Frustration and hurt pulsed through his body. After a few moments, he asked, "Then what do you want me to do?"

She said sternly, "I want you to clean the sheep barn." At that moment, B.J. had to make a decision. Would he submit to her spiritual wisdom and authority or pursue what he considered the opportunity of a lifetime? With his head down and his shoulders sloped, he got up and walked to the sheep barn. For the next six hours, by himself, he did nothing but clean. But, God was also cleansing. While B.J. worked on the stalls, God worked on his soul. B.J. recounts:

Strangely, after a couple hours of battling, an unexplained joy descended on my soul. I knew that I needed to learn to submit. I knew I needed to follow the counsel. In that sheep's barn, the Shepherd met me. He sheared the wool from my eyes, and I am eternally grateful. I look back over three decades and sing His praises for my decision to submit. My heart mattered to my Lord far and above my ministry for my Lord. If I had not learned to submit, as you say "respectfully doing what was rightfully required of me" when I did not want to do it, I do not believe my ministry in New York on the streets with the poor and the prostitutes, and then onto Wall Street with the prosperous and the professionals, or with athletes, would have lasted.

Choosing to submit to Jesus in the face of temptations and trials and willfulness, I was learning obedience mucking sheep's manure off a smelly stall floor, doing what I was supposed to do, not what I wanted to do. That moment of obedience and submission opened unique doors far greater than Billy Graham's Cincinnati Crusade, as significant as that event proved to be for others.[1]

Rebels need to hear B.J.'s testimony, especially those who are ambitious, highly concerned about status, and disgruntled by delays. While eventually many of these rebels rise to leadership positions, God often tames them through the discipline of submission so that they do not mess up future opportunities. Scripture warns that when you make wrong choices early on, refusing to submit to God's ways, then "you groan at your final end" (Proverbs 5:11).

It is a simple principle of leadership: If I haven't learned to submit to authority as a follower, when I am a leader I will abuse my authority, and God knows this.

But what if the person over us in authority does not have our best interests at heart, or so we feel this way?

What about Frustrations with Unreasonable Authority?

In 1 Peter 2:13–16, Peter focuses our attention on what God does when we face unfair treatment. Indeed, some of us suffer because an authority figure treats us harshly for no good reason. Though they do not demand that we do evil, they make our life miserable because of who they are.

The good news is that "God is pleased with you when you do what you know is right and patiently endure unfair treatment" (1 Peter 2:19 NLT). We get God's attention. Two times Peter writes: "For this finds favor, . . ." and, "This finds favor with God" (1 Peter 2:19–20). Peter clearly tells his readers that God sees and extends grace, kindness, and blessing to the mistreated.

We must never lose sight of this.

Frustrations with an Employer

One time when I spoke in Colorado Springs, a man named Jeff picked me up at the airport. When I learned that he had been on the faculty at the Air Force Academy, I broached the subject of submission at the Academy. To my surprise, he shifted the focus to himself and shared how he learned to submit during his early years in business.

Jeff recounted the dilemma he faced when God put it in his heart to leave his job and serve Him elsewhere. Because Jeff had made a promise to his unbelieving employer to continue working for him for years, he felt morally obligated to stay. As he spent more time in prayer, Jeff knew God was leading him to leave; but he also felt the Lord telling him to remain employed with this gentleman. In his confusion, he asked the Lord what he should do. The Lord revealed to him that he should, "Submit to this man." Jeff contested, "But I feel You're leading me away." "Yes," the Lord responded, "but submit."

Jeff knew that if he left the business, this unbelieving boss would use the broken promise against him and his testimony for Christ. Unfortunately, we can find ourselves in situations like Jeff's. We are held to a higher standard because we are believers in Christ. We feel a pressure and unfair treatment because we cannot just up and quit due to the discredit this could bring to the name of Christ. It isn't just about us. Like Jeff, we feel bound and trapped. Jeff did not feel he had any other option than to submit to the job and continue working, which he did for a lengthy period of time. During all that time, he said nothing to his boss about his inner stirrings to leave, since he knew his boss would throw that in his face. Jeff could only pray and patiently endure this sorrowful situation. For Jeff and many of us, few things rub us the wrong way and wear us out like our work situation. We feel stuck.

One day, out of the blue, the boss asked in a way contrary to his character, "Jeff, what would you like to do if you didn't work here?" Stunned, Jeff could not believe what he was hearing. The incongruity of that question with the daily content of conversation from his boss was astonishing! Composing himself, Jeff haltingly voiced his secret aspirations. The boss replied, "You know, Jeff, I've been thinking about you, and that's why I asked. I think you ought to do that. And as for that obligation, it's off the table. I don't want to lose you, but I believe you should do what you just told me."

Jeff learned that day that obedience to the universal will of God on submission leads to an experience of the unique will of God. As Jeff submitted to his boss, he began to see the favor of God working itself out in his employment.

Frustrations with a Parent

Jeff got so excited about the power of submission that he asked the Lord to reveal more to him about the way it works. This time the Lord spoke to his heart, "Go seek your father's forgiveness for not having been a good, submissive son." Shocked, Jeff told the Lord, "But he was a horrible dad and did not deserve my submission and respect." The Lord said to him, "Right now, your dad is not my concern. My concern is with your past disobedience and rebellion. I want you to seek your father's forgiveness." Jeff fought the Lord for a period of time; but eventually he went to his dad and said, "Dad, I was not a respectful and submissive son. I rebelled against your authority. Will you forgive me?"

His dad did forgive him, but nothing seemed to change in his father. But what blew me away is what Jeff said next, "After I did this with my dad, a weight lifted from my shoulders that I did not know was there and a peace descended upon my soul that I did not know was not there."

Wow! We are back to the "presence of God" we addressed in chapter 2.

Some of you don't know what you are missing because you are depriving yourself of the glorious rewards connected to submission. Don't be like the farmer who had to keep a 2x4 ready to hit his mule upside of his head. When another farmer said, "That won't get him to move," the first farmer replied, "I am not trying to get him to move. I am trying to get his attention." Is God using authorities as a 2x4 to get your attention? Does He intend for you to see the favor He will bring when you respectfully do what is rightly required of you?

In short, are you paying attention? Or, are you holding back? One young man heard me tell Jeff's story. Shortly thereafter, he wrote: "After hearing your sermon, I jotted down a note about Jeff apologizing to his father. There have been times when I felt led to write something out to my dad, but have never gotten around to it. I believe I have forgiven him in my heart, but I have not asked him for forgiveness for not submitting to his authority." I believe this young man is missing out on God's favor coming to him because he is holding back. Sometimes the first act of submission is seeking forgiveness for failing to submit.

Let me add one word of caution: Not everyone who submits to authority necessarily submits to God. Some folks possess a compliant personality and have no faith in God. Not everyone, therefore, who follows the orders of an authority figure encounters God. But, every believer who really encounters God will learn to submit to authority.

Frustrations in Marriage

To close this chapter, I believe it is finally time to address this controversial topic of submission in marriage.

In Ephesians 5:21 we read of mutual submission: "be subject to one another." Paul then goes on to instruct wives to submit to their husbands (vv. 22–24) and husbands to love their wives (vv. 25–29). He then summarizes the passage on marriage in verse 33 by instructing husbands to love their wives and wives to respect their husbands. If a wife's submission is central, why does he say nothing of submission in his summary verse, calling wives instead to respect their husbands? Simple. A wife submits by meeting her husband's need for respect. A husband submits to—or is "subject to"—his wife's need for love.

Frustrations with a Husband

The apostle Peter concurs with Paul on this teaching. In 1 Peter 3:1–2, Peter instructs wives to submit to their husbands by meeting a husband's need to feel respected. He adds the encouragement that her "respectful behavior" (v. 2) can win a disobedient husband. Is there any greater favor? Yes, submission is hard; but, as Peter declares, it always finds "favor" with God. He writes, "be submissive" for "when you do what is right and suffer for it" and "patiently endure it, this finds favor with God" (1 Peter 2:18–20).

Listen to this story of a wife who learned the power of submitting to her husband's need for respect. She testifies:

> Two and a half years ago I went from nominal Christian to a full-time lover of Jesus. However, my marriage was falling apart. My husband disliked being around me. He didn't talk to me for days on end. He said numerous times that we were too different and that once the kids (four and six at the time) were grown we would need to separate. Since my marriage was in tatters, I read what God had to say. Being schooled in the feminist camp, I found the words "submissive" and "submit" in 1 Peter 3:1 and Ephesians 5:22 very difficult to swallow. However, I knew that I could not argue with the first real Love that I was experiencing, so I gave over to 1 Peter 3:1. I had not been putting my husband, Raj, first. I had to start focusing on home more. When my husband said something, I tried to honor his words.

Over time, the difference in this wife's submissive attitude became apparent to her husband. Though he initially harbored a skeptical attitude about the genuineness of her faith and changes in attitude, God's work in her began to win his favor. She explains:

> The love of Jesus was so full in me that I really was completely fine. I was in a euphoric place for about six months after I became a Christian, and my husband was watching me and wondering when it would end. I had a reason to submit: to win him, as 1 Peter 3:1 said. After a while his demeanor

changed toward me—he started to like me, said kind things to me, wanted to be around me. Then I heard a piece of your conference on the radio and it blew me away. I was flabbergasted. It was God's amazing timing. The whole submit thing became easier to swallow once you described it as meeting a man's need for respect. Then it all started to make sense. I was no longer doing it without knowing. I started to use the word *respect* around him, and it solidified his turn-around. Respect was the *huge* key to him letting down his guard to trusting me and thereby trusting Jesus and letting Him in.

Though she admits that her husband's path to Jesus took a while, she describes a moment when she needed to draw the line with him on his habitual pornography viewing. Since submission and respect never mean giving license for a spouse to do evil, this wife confronted her husband respectfully, saying she could not continue in the relationship with him if he stayed connected to this form of adultery. Eventually, she says, "he broke and let God in. He is now completely changed and won over." God's favor to her for her submission is so apparent that she confesses:

I don't even *recognize* the man I married. He is *completely* different. After thirteen years I can finally say our marriage is truly like a dream. It is unbelievable how tender and fun and honest and caring and loving and joyful and playful and kind and intimate and generous and forgiving and sincere and giving and wonderful our marriage is. It is a *miracle*. My husband has embraced Jesus I truly believe as a direct result of Ephesians 5:22 and 1 Peter 3:1.[2]

Don't miss the foundational point here. In this wife's time of marital crisis and suffering, she opened her heart totally to the Lord and found His favor. The power of her encounter with God released her to submit to her husband and triggered great change in their marriage. Notice again how she describes His power with the joyful words: "the first real love I was experiencing," "the love of Jesus was full in me," "I was in a euphoric state," "and God's timing was amazing." Submission is less about the horizontal and more about the vertical. Each of us must let Christ have His way in our hearts and when we do, He favors us in the midst of our suffering. Again, submission to God's universal will leads to unique blessings in each individual life.

Frustrations with a Wife

What about husbands who submit to God's plan to love their wives? Do they also find God's favor? Yes, and this is especially true during a conflict when a wife shows disrespect (Ephesians 5:21, 25, 33). Remember, "When you do what is right and suffer for it" and "you patiently endure it, this finds favor with God" (1 Peter 2:20). But, note what Peter specifically calls husbands to do: "You husbands in the same way, live with your wives in an understanding way, as with someone weaker, since she is a woman; and show her honor as a fellow heir of the grace of life, so that your prayers will not be hindered" (1 Peter 3:7).

Many strong, talented women balk at the word "weaker" and miss the fact that the phrase "in the same way" refers to the concept of submission. In the section from 1 Peter 2:13–3:7, Peter addresses three relationships that require submission, and husbands are to submit in the same way that citizens, slaves, and wives submit. A picture of this is provided by Paul when he shows that a husband submits by loving his wife (Ephesians 5:21, 25) and Peter describes it as understanding his wife as a woman, and honoring her as an equal (1 Peter 3:7).

What is the reward for the husband who submits to loving, understanding, and honoring his wife in this way? According to 1 Peter 3:7, God will answer his prayers. Talk about God's favor! This man's prayers will not be hindered!

Listen to this story of a husband we will call Tim, who sought after his adulterous wife and worked to win her back with love much like Hosea in the Old Testament (Hosea 3:1). Though Tim owns that his lack of love for his wife contributed to her unfaithfulness, he found God's favor when he submitted to her need for his love.

> About once or twice a year we'd have a big argument where she would give me the laundry list of all the things I was doing wrong and ask why I hated her. I was always surprised—I thought I loved her very much. By biting the bullet and not

letting her emasculating behaviors toward me affect me, I thought I was being the bigger, better man. In reality, I was the king of the stonewall. The only time I would show her any tenderness at all was when I wanted to have sex . . . which was constantly . . . so I thought I was showing love on a regular basis. She became desperate for me to love her, which I thought I did. Only now do I realize that my behavior was telling her just the opposite.

By God's grace several things happened that helped turn this marriage around. The first was that Tim "came to understand that [his] wife had been having an affair for a couple of months." As he says, "This rocked my world. It never occurred to me that she would ever cheat on me. This devastated me."

The next thing that intervened in their marital crisis was a visit to his in-laws where Tim discovered a copy of my book *Love & Respect* sitting on the table. Through the book, Tim says that he came to the realization, "I had failed in my greatest task—to love my wife as Christ loves the church. Never before in our marriage had I seen how *my* behavior was affecting my wife." Looking back, he can now see that he never believed his wife when she said things like, "Why do you hate me?" Because he had never said those words to her in his life, he thought she must be "crazy."

After reading the book, many of Tim's perspectives were altered. He says, "I now see how my stonewalling and my hard and closed-off heart gave her exactly that message. I was selfish, hard-hearted, and closed." Once he unpacked this, he says, "I hit my knees and begged God for the grace to change and the grace to forgive her. And boy did He ever grant that. I've never understood the idea of 'the fervent prayers of a righteous man avails much' until that moment. I prayed, and the Lord answered my prayers. The wall of stone around my heart was crushed and broken. Armed with the knowledge from your book, I began to love my wife the way I should have been doing for the last ten years."

Though Tim's wife had decided to leave because "she just couldn't take it anymore," he won her back by his submission to love her even though both had been deeply hurt. He told me, "I have learned to love by serving. For example, my wife and I have started cooking together, and it's one of the best parts of our day. Not only have I been open and soft-hearted with her, but she has been a *completely* different person toward me. I see now how my behavior affected her." God favors the husband who humbles himself like this. Submitting to his wife's need for love elevates a man in his home. God will hear such a man and work great things in his life and the life of his wife. So, husbands, when you think of submission, think of God's favor!

Let's Remember the Eternal Perspective

In all of this discussion, there is an eternal perspective we need to keep in mind. The incentive for doing such submissive acts of service arises from God's announcement of what awaits us in heaven. "Well done, good and faithful servant! You have been faithful with a few things; I will put you in charge of many things. Come and share your master's happiness" (Matthew 25:21 NIV). Servants submit to the wishes and requirements of others in authority over them. Every time we respectfully do what is rightfully required of us, as submissive and respectful servants, we demonstrate to our watching Lord that we are good and faithful servants. Ironically, though we are not in charge nor always happy, our submissive service directly contributes to us living happily ever after in heaven. We are put in charge of many glorious things throughout eternity. This is mind-boggling. Though heaven is a free gift through faith in Christ, what God promises to give us in heaven for our faithful service exceeds our finite mind's ability to fathom this. Yet, we get a glimpse, and this sneak peak makes us less frightened about serving those over us. In the deepest sense we "submit . . . for the Lord's sake" as Peter teaches (1 Peter 2:13). We do what we do unto Christ who will reward us on that Day. The Lord takes notice. Everything matters and counts to Him. We must never lose sight of the fact that the Lord never loses sight of us.

"Okay, Emerson, I am thrilled with the prospects of submission on Earth and in heaven. But I feel like some authority ought to be resisted since blind submission is idiotic. There are bad authorities out there. We need to question authority!"

Let's consider in the next chapter some reasons people feel resistance to authority is for their good.

Chapter 8
RESISTANCE TO SUBMISSION

Why do some people resist the idea of submission? They think the following:

- We should live and let live; submitting to rules is unnecessary.
- Submitters are second-class, whereas entrepreneurs are first-class.
- Freedom from authority reduces hardship.
- Submission leads to abuse.
- Submission prevents rightful civil disobedience.
- Biblical submission justifies slavery.
- Submission prevents praying against authorities.
- Submission emboldens bad people.
- Submitting by righting our wrong is foolish.

We Should Live and Let Live; Submitting to Rules Is Unnecessary

I went to military school from eighth grade to twelfth grade. For five years, I rose at 6:20 every morning hearing the trumpeter play reveille and went to bed at 9:45 each evening hearing the trumpeter play taps. I can tell you the routine for every hour of every day. I stood at attention. I marched.

I saluted. I said, "Yes sir." During those years, someone ranked above me would require me to respectfully fulfill my duties. I lived in submission.

I can tell you this, someone might be born to lead, but no one is born to submit! That's why God commands it.

Yes, the word *submit* unsettles even those who consider themselves law-abiding. It makes us want to ask why, and when, and to whom. I can remember my anger at military school when the president of the Academy gave me a demerit for not wearing my hat while off campus. In uniform, but hatless, I walked twenty feet from my parents' car to enter a restaurant. Surely, that was not a cause for a demerit! However, the Academy had established a rule in the 1800s (wear your hat when outside); and in order for those in authority to lead justly, they needed to apply the rules consistently. Why make an exception with me? Yet, I considered myself an exception. My anger surged. "What is the big deal?" *Not wearing my hat off campus is pretty petty stuff*, I thought. What difference could it make? But the President of the Academy saw me firsthand and reported me.

But according to military thinking, the difference between scrupulous obedience and independent thinking could ultimately mean life or death on a battlefield. If we don't learn obedience in the little things, we may not be ready when it counts.

Someone objects, "Emerson, submissive people are unthinking and go along with Vietnam, Iraq, and all unjust wars. 'Question Authority!'"

To an extent, I agree. There are unthinking people herded about like dumb sheep. But at this juncture I am not talking about civil disobedience in the face of inhumane requirements. I am not waxing eloquent about just war theory. I am talking about my rebellious spirit for the demerit I received for not wearing my hat. This was my issue and I tried to make it Colonel Stribling's issue. Emotionally, I felt he was unfair for disciplining me. I felt the rule was unnecessary and we should live and let live. This was no big deal in my opinion. There are more important things. That's why I was shocked and angered when I saw my name posted on the bulletin board for receiving a demerit.

But the truth was I didn't want to obey the rule because at that moment it seemed superfluous. However, in any military operation or organization, rules are required that are not moral issues per se but functional matters. The Academy asked, "In the overall scheme of things, should a cadet ever be outside without a hat?" The Academy decided the simplest and easiest rule was to say, "No."

At the time, though, I wished to argue the unfairness of that demerit. As a teenager I had moments—can you imagine—wherein I was arrogant, self-centered, and a know-it-all. I would have enjoyed holding up the sign, "Question Authority!" But in this setting on this matter, I was wrong. Almost all rules have a reasonable basis to them.

Yes, I often joke that some church policies are created in response to one negative experience that caught the church leadership off guard so they make a rule to prevent that from ever happening again until someone asks thirty years later, "Why do we have this policy in place?" For example, a pulpit guest said something that sounded unbiblical, so the board created a rule that every speaker be vetted. So when someone like Billy Graham was asked to speak years later, he had to submit his statement of faith in writing and be interviewed. The rule seems silly, though the motive was to prevent the church from being subjected to heresy!

But we are not addressing the rule that is the exception, and which calls for us to make an exception to this rule! Instead, we are addressing the idea that rules related to showing up to work at a certain time, taking a break and lunch at a certain time, showing up at the meeting on time, handing in the project on time, returning from a two-week vacation at the end of two weeks, etc., allow for an organization to be as fair as possible to all involved. Most rules—and there can be hundreds of such rules—are reasonable, efficient, and effective in moving the organization forward in achieving its mission.

It makes perfect sense why everyone in the organization (a place that's organized), should submit to the rules. To live and let live leads to chaos and disorganization. To say rules are unnecessary sounds nice when arguing one need not wear a hat for twenty seconds outside. However, as I look back now, if I were head of the Academy, I'd make the same rule. It is part of the military uniform, and making an exception here and there will only lead to unnecessary contentions and wasted time in debating new exceptions. That rule—always wear your hat when outside—is not unreasonable, but efficient and wise, given hats are part of a uniform. It eliminates debate. It makes no difference if you are outside for twenty hours or twenty seconds. Wear the hat. It is fair to all, keeping the organization uniformed.

While the course of history seems punctuated by the legacy of evil men and regimes, rarely in our daily existence do we find ourselves pitted against authority figures requiring us to do evil. Most of the time when we rebel against what we consider "bad authorities," it is because we find the rule stupid and unfair and we have a better way to do it. We don't like the demands of the leader so we deem them "bad." But can we honestly say that what he or she is requiring us to do is something bad, or for that matter, they are bad leaders for having us do what we deem unnecessary? At military school no one ever asked me to do anything bad. However, I did not like the unappetizing and inconvenient requirements that came at me day after day. I had to shine my shoes—again. I had to clean my room—again. I had to make my bed—again. I had to get up—again. However, none of these rules required me to disobey God. They just required me to do, with a respectful attitude, things I didn't want to do. Furthermore, when I or anyone else got in trouble, it was due to a violation of a clear rule that everyone else had to follow. In that sense, the rule was fair. When we got into trouble, it was because we made wrong choices.

Some of us need to get in tune with why we oppose the concept of submission. Are we being required to submit to a rule that we feel is unnecessary? Or, in the overall scheme of things, does the rule make the best sense for the institution and is it fair to all? Let's be honest. Too often our real problem with the rule is that it inconveniences us, like I was inconvenienced when required to wear my hat outside for twenty seconds, after I had combed my hair to go into the restaurant. Putting the hat on messed up my hair—what little hair I had as a cadet!

Submitters Are Second-Class Whereas Entrepreneurs Are First-Class

My daughter Joy writes, "Not too long ago I spoke at a university's chapel. After the event was finished, some of the students came up to speak to me. One guy came up and very formally shook my hand. He told me that he was part of the 'Entrepreneurial Club' and thought I did an excellent job. The conversation went something like this:

"Thank you. I appreciate that."

"Have you ever considered doing something on your own?"

"What do you mean?"

"Well, you mentioned working for your parents, but I think you have enough talent to go out on your own."

"(Laughing) That's very kind of you to say, but I enjoy working for my parents. That is the whole reason I do what I do, because I believe in their message and want to get it to our generation."

"But wouldn't you want to have your own thing?"

"No. I think it's very healthy to have the covering of wise counsel over us, especially at a young age. I want them as my boss."

"But you could be your own boss!"

She continued. "He was trying to sell me some glorious life, free of 'the boss man.' It was an honor to think that he thought I was talented, and I guess he was just trying to do his job as an entrepreneur scouting out his next 'thing,' but it got me thinking about what we value as the best position to be in."

What do you think?

Being an entrepreneur has many advantages in freeing us up to chase after the dream we believe God has for us. Sometimes companies are not compatible with our vision. We can operate more independently, and one should not feel guilty about working for oneself. Just as we are free to direct our own steps as we follow the four wills of God, so we are free to be entrepreneurs based on our interest, talent, and opportunity. As long as we don't compromise the four wills of God, we are free.

On the other hand, we must recognize that we can never be totally free of authority since we will have to submit to the laws of the land, like paying taxes. Besides, when our vision can be filled with satisfaction within a company, submission includes the opportunity to achieve the mission we value.

Some wrongly think that independence from authority leads to greater freedom. Actually, more freedom could be gained within institutions.

Over the years many have told me that as they worked for a company, there were more benefits than if they launched out on their own. As they weighed the pros and cons of leaving versus staying, their cost-benefit analysis caused them to conclude that staying put gave them more advantages. Even though they had to submit to a chain of command that could frustrate them, the structure also gave them resources, rights, and privileges. For instance, these people would say, "If I started my own company, I would have to provide the medical coverage for myself and my employees. Though I might have greater freedom of working my own hours or from home, I realized that I would be chained to a legal obligation of providing health insurance."

Some people think that any type of submission demands that we "bow to the man." Such a metaphor can overlook all that "the man" provides. Good organizations intend to keep good help. Some leaders put golden handcuffs on trustworthy and competent workers. Yes, there are rules and regulations, but the trade-off can be worth it.

My daughter addresses the intangibles we receive under authorities. She says, "I realize some of you have awful bosses, and some of you work for yourselves and it's fantastic. I get that. But for me, in my life, my parents happen to be wise people and also my bosses. Therefore, I have entrusted them to 'oversee me' in quite a few areas. For you, it may not be your boss or your parents, but when you look at your life, do you have any overseers? . . . It's no mystery that we live in a generation where most of us are free to pick up and move and live independently of our parents. To actually have authority figures in our lives is something we would have to seek out . . . unless of course you were assigned your most recent parole officer. I believe we have glorified independence as if that is the best way to live. We have 'bucked the system,' said 'down with the man.'. . . When I sit back and write that out, I shake my head at its sheer stupidity. It's my nature to look at people younger than myself and point out how foolish they are, and yet when someone older tells me I'm doing something wrong, I'm quick to dub them ignorant idiots . . . but I think we need to reevaluate why we think independence is so great . . . My mother is almost sixty and would be the first to say she doesn't have life figured out. So in my opinion, community and accountability and having 'overseers' doesn't mean we blindly follow anyone who is in AARP, but it means mutually learning from one another, accepting differences, and seeking out people who have gone before us and humbly submitting to some level of authority. When I start believing that the pinnacle of life is independence and no one 'telling me what to do,' my guess is I will stop growing and stop gaining wisdom. And as sad as that is, the bigger question I must ask myself is this: If I am not humble enough to come under the authority of any human being, what makes me think that I would be humble enough to come under the authority of God?"

Freedom from Authority Reduces Hardship

You may have heard the statement, "I have been poor and I have been rich. Rich is better." In a sense, that's true. Proverbs 10:15 states, "The rich man's wealth is his fortress, the ruin of the poor is their poverty." Wealth protects us.

Another common expression is, "He is independently wealthy." We do not say "she is independently beautiful or athletic." Riches enable us to be independent of the normal hassles of life, especially from bothersome authority figures.

However, as my daughter Joy stated, there is another side to this equation. I know of one wealthy person who, when confronted with things about their horrible personality that needed changing, moved away to a bigger mansion in another city and started over in that community with immediate status due to their wealth. Obviously the wealthy can live independent of people who confront their character flaws. The hardships that most of us face when corrected for a bad attitude can be escaped by the independently wealthy. They can flee the rebuke—at least for a while. John Donne penned, "No man is an island entire of itself." We can never be absolutely free from everyone and everything. We are not a law unto ourselves, nor above the law. Heartaches and headaches come to all of us.

We can mislead ourselves into concluding that freedom from authority reduces all hardship. Proverbs 18:11 states, "A rich man's wealth is his strong city, and like a high wall in his own imagination." For instance, rich people eventually submit to dying and death, and to imagine otherwise is utter foolishness. There is no U-Haul behind a hearse. As the Bible says, naked we came into this world and naked we will leave. Freedom has its limits.

Rich and poor alike have a common humanity. James 1:10 states, "the rich man . . . like flowering grass . . . will pass away." Truth be told, the rich have no more staying power than grass. And when we stand before God's judgment, wealth will be irrelevant (Proverbs 11:4).

In the book of James we learn that trials come to all of us. He lists numerous trials: humiliating circumstances (1:9–10), angry brethren (1:19), lonesome distress (1:27), favoritism (2:1), dishonor for poorness (2:6), neglected necessities (2:15–16), verbal curses (3:1–12; see especially v. 10), another's bitter jealousy (3:14, 16), quarrels and conflicts (4:1–2), unanswered prayers (4:3), God's opposition to pride (4:6, 10), judgmental brethren (4:11), thwarted business plans (4:13–17), miseries though wealthy (5:1–6), withheld pay (5:4), condemnation and death (5:6), waiting, waiting, waiting (5:7–11), another's false "yes" or "no" (5:12), suffering and sickness (5:13–14), and straying loved ones (5:19–20).

All Christ-followers—those seeking to follow His universal and unique will for our lives—will face frustrations and stresses, whether independently wealthy or not.

Even if we gained freedom from all human authority, we are always under the authority and law of Christ (1 Corinthians 9:21), and this is never easy street. As the four wills state:

- We must still believe in and behold Jesus Christ who is Lord over us. We are slaves of Christ. We are not our own bosses. We were bought with a price.
- We must abstain from sexual impurity under the holiness and lordship of Christ. How many put this book down the minute they saw this will of God?
- We must give thanks to Him when we do not have the power to work all things together for good, and border on letting ourselves become resentful over the mistreatment.
- We must submit to the laws of Christ in doing what is right when that costs us, especially when we could have done wrong and no one would have known.

Does the Bible actually use the word *hardship* for those following Christ? Anyone reading the book of Acts and the Epistles recognizes what happened to the apostle Paul as he followed the will of God and sought to help others follow His purpose.

"I have been in labor and hardship, through many sleepless nights, in hunger and thirst, often without food, in cold and exposure." (2 Corinthians 11:27)

"For you recall, brethren, our labor and hardship, how working night and day so as not to be a burden to any of you, we proclaimed to you the gospel of God." (1 Thessalonians 2:9)

"Nor did we eat anyone's bread without paying for it, but with labor and hardship we kept working night and day so that we would not be a burden to any of you." (2 Thessalonians 3:8)

"For which I suffer hardship even to imprisonment as a criminal; but the word of God is not imprisoned." (2 Timothy 2:9)

Paul tells us that we too must be prepared for these challenges.

"Suffer hardship with me, as a good soldier of Christ Jesus." (2 Timothy 2:3)

"But you, be sober in all things, endure hardship, do the work of an evangelist, fulfill your ministry." (2 Timothy 4:5)

Some of us mistakenly think that when God personally directs our steps, He will lead us to a place of near paradise where everyone loves and respects us, and responds to our love and respect. Of course, when that doesn't happen, we get hurt and frustrated, and some question God's leading. Though He opened a door so big one could fishtail a Mack truck through it, after entering the door, God allows trials. How many of us hear from people exclaiming their awe over God's direction of their lives to do such and such only to hear a year later, "Oh, that didn't work out"? Why is this? Did God change His mind? Unfortunately, this person was not mature enough to keep on respectfully doing what was rightly required of them. It got too tough and they quit. This serves as a reminder to each of us that when we submit to God's four wills, we must prepare for tough times. The idea that we ought to pursue freedom from authority with a vengeance in order to reduce hardships or that God's will removes difficulties overlooks reality and the Bible.

Submission Leads to Abuse

Whenever I speak on this command to submit, someone surfaces, "But what about evil people, like an uncle who molests his niece? You aren't saying she should submit to her uncle's sexual abuse, are you?"

The one asking the question knows I am not saying this, but they are asking what we all ask, "Where is the line to be drawn on submission?"

The news is full of such wicked examples. The staggering statistics regarding spouse and child abuse, incest, and pedophilia (even among religious leaders), remind us that abuses of authority scars many in domestic life. Similar abuses of power abound in business and political domains. A year does not seem to go by without exposure of yet another leader who has cheated the trusting public by illegal or immoral practices.

The stories of submission in the previous chapter examine generally well-meaning authorities. But, how should we respond if we suffer under a truly evil authority figure?

Nothing in 1 Peter 2:13–15 remotely suggests we must submit to wrongdoing. If an uncle is sexually abusing a niece, the niece needs to report this to the police or a medical doctor who are authorities themselves and can protect the innocent niece. Taking a stand, as risky as this might be, is important to prevent this abuser from sexually violating others. If you are a young person reading this and find yourself being abused, you must be brave and turn to other authority figures for help. As Peter taught, the king and governors are there "for the punishment of evildoers" (1 Peter 2:13–15). Though matters of abuse are beyond the scope of this book, *you must never interpret the concept of submission to mean submission to evil acts. That is contrary to the heart and will of God.*

Biblical submission never sanctions giving into evil, but turning over such abusers to the authorities "for the punishment of evildoers."

Submission Prevents Civil Disobedience

You must distinguish between "bad authorities"—those who do evil by expecting you to do things contrary to the law of God—and those who are just "bad at" leading. God calls you to submit to the latter, but He does not call you to submit to the evildoer, as we just said. On the contrary, you may well be called to expose his or her evildoing (Ephesians 5:11). Thus, you will need to take a stand and suffer the consequences. Civil disobedience may be demanded.

Peter would never instruct us to submit to acting contrary to the four wills of God. He himself did not submit when told to act in opposition to the words of Christ (Acts 4:19; 5:29).

Peter was convinced that you must never disobey what God has called you to do. Though Peter teaches submission (1 Peter 2:13–15), he shows in his own life a place for civil disobedience. Observe Peter and John in the book of Acts: "And when they had summoned them, they commanded them not to speak or teach at all in the name of Jesus. But Peter and John answered and said to them, 'Whether it is right in the sight of God to give heed to you rather than to God, you be the judge'" (Acts 4:18–19). Later we read, "'We gave you strict orders not to continue teaching in this name, and yet, you have filled Jerusalem with your teaching and intend to bring this man's blood upon us.' But Peter and the apostles answered: 'We must obey God rather than men'" (Acts 5:28–29). Peter understood that his commitment to follow God's command to him superseded all else.

I believe that when Christ-followers enter civil disobedience, they do so with the full recognition that they might suffer the consequences of that decision. When we decide to obey God rather than man, we must prepare to be hammered with the full weight of the erring authorities. Martin Luther King Jr. resisted the authorities in making his case against them, but he did so in a humble spirit that eventually proved winsome to a watching world. However, when the authorities arrested him, he submitted to jail time instead of resisting in violence. For instance, in 1963, the court ordered him not to protest the treatment of African-Americans in Birmingham, Alabama, and when he did, they sent him to jail. Of course, there he penned the famous "Letter from Birmingham Jail."

Another story involving Peter is most telling. Though Peter calls wives to submit to their husbands (1 Peter 3:1), what Peter says to one particular wife (Acts 5) shows that he expects wives to draw a line in the sand when it comes to going along with their husbands who lie. In Acts 5, Ananias and Sapphira had agreed together to lie to God and the early church about the amount of money they gave to the church from a piece of property they sold.

Earlier, another person, Barnabas, had sold a piece of property and given the money to the church. Because the early believers had pooled their resources, what Barnabas did caused everyone to be encouraged and filled with praise (Acts 4:34–37). Apparently, Ananias and Sapphira wanted to be praised like Barnabas but did not want to make the same sacrifice Barnabas made, so they came up with a deceptive plan to get the church's praise while keeping back a large amount of money for themselves. For example, they might have sold the property for $250,000 but said they sold it for $150,000, and kept back $100,000 for themselves, maybe breaking even on their original investment. But when giving the $150,000 they told everyone that they were giving it all, to the last penny, to the church. The Lord disciplined Ananias by ending his life over this sin. Several hours later, Peter makes inquiry of Sapphira, who continues to tell the lie. She does not come clean. So, does Peter praise her for her submission to Ananias? Do we hear Peter praising her, "Oh, Sapphira, you were a submissive, respectful wife who went along with the evil plan of your husband, therefore you get to go free because of this submissive attitude"? No way. Peter rebukes her for lying to the Holy Spirit, and she dies on the spot. Peter expected everyone who submits to submit within godly boundaries.

When Paul writes in Ephesians 5:24 (NIV), "Now as the church submits to Christ, so also wives should submit to their husbands in everything," what does Paul mean by "everything"? Are there no exceptions? He explains his meaning in Colossians. "Wives, be subject to your husbands, as is fitting in the Lord" (3:18). In other words, there are boundaries—submit in everything that is fitting in the Lord! One's submission should not run contrary to what Christ would do, and Paul assumes we know what is fitting as one called to follow Christ.

Few things are as daunting as standing your ground or standing up to an immoral or illegal authority figure. In the case of Sapphira, Peter did not expect her to submit for the Lord's sake to Ananias. Instead, she was to submit by respectfully informing him that she would not lie before God and the church about the price of the property. Hopefully, she could appeal to Ananias's honorable side and say, "Let's make the same sacrifice Barnabas did and trust God together." If Ananias refused, Sapphira would need to humbly but courageously side with Christ, doing only what was fitting in the Lord. Paul is clear, "Do not participate in the unfruitful deeds of darkness, but instead even expose them"

(Ephesians 5:11). If need be, she might have to physically separate from her husband (1 Corinthians 7:11) in the event he turned abusive, and then with a broken heart come to Peter and report Ananias's plan.

As for us, ideally, if your boss requests you to do something illegal or immoral, he will retract his demand when you take a humble but firm stand. Once we draw a line in the sand about not conspiring with them, most back-pedal. Yes, there is a price to pay in terms of them not liking you, but that's better than you not liking yourself because you compromised your convictions and conscience, and forfeited God's favor.

Again, there are hierarchical structures in most situations. Appealing to a higher authority in the company (or family) about someone else's abuse of authority is appropriate. That's why God has established authority in the government and church. Even in Rome in the first century, there were authorities overseeing other authorities. God has designed checks and balances in most situations, even in troubling regimes.

However, all of us must be prepared to obey God, not man, when authorities demand of us to live in such a way that we deny the four wills of God.

Will we believe in Jesus Christ no matter what? No authority has the right to tell us to stop believing in Jesus. We must stand firm, as they did, for instance, in Philippi. There, in the first century, the Christians were told that they could believe in Jesus Christ but they must also bow to Caesar and the gods. If they did not worship Caesar, they would later be ushered into the arena to be eaten by the lions. Many chose martyrdom. Worshipping Caesar and Christ was not possible. They took a stand.

Will we abstain from sexual sin no matter what? Many of us live in environments where the people who have the influence expect us to participate in acts that are unholy, like sex, drugs, and excessive drinking. When we refuse, they make our lives miserable. Will we remain obedient to God and disobedient to these sensual leaders? In a sense, this is a form of civil disobedience.

Will we give thanks to God no matter what? There are cynics among the influencers in our lives who mock us when we give thanks to God during bad and stressful times. They tell us there is no God or that we ought to curse God for the awful things happening to us. Will we remain thankful though these folks think us fools and mistreat us? Though we need not wear our religion on our sleeve, do we keep on trusting and thanking God no matter the rejection we encounter from those over us?

Will we submit in doing what is right? Some of us find ourselves in situations where the protocol is to do wrong given one can get away with it. The influencers equate shrewdness with artful deceptions. Will we stand firm and continue to do what is right in the face of those who attack us for doing the right thing when it was to our advantage to do the wrong thing?

When corrupt authority does not back down, will we?

Biblical Submission Justifies Slavery

Some people claim that it is abhorrent that the Bible supports and sanctions slavery. However, that is not so. The Bible recognizes the reality of slavery but does not endorse it. If people read all of the Bible they'd come across 1 Corinthians 7:21, written to slaves: "if you are able also to become free, rather do that." The apostle Paul did not approve of slavery but encouraged slaves to pursue freedom where they could. However, his other concern was to help those slaves who could not gain their freedom. He cast a vision that everything they did for Christ, though the slaves of men, would be rewarded by God. Paul took their eyes off the horizontal bondage and instilled an understanding of God's Kingdom. "Slaves, be obedient . . . in the sincerity of your heart, as to Christ; not by way of eyeservice, as men-pleasers, but as slaves of Christ, doing the will of God from the heart. With good will render service, as to the Lord, and not to men, knowing that whatever good thing each one does, this he will receive back from the Lord, whether slave or free" (Ephesians 6:5–8). Paul inspires slaves to believe that Jesus Christ will reward them for everything they do unto Him. Nothing is wasted.

For us, we may not be slaves, but we are indentured laborers. The word to us is that if we can leave, and feel that we should, then we can freely leave. We can seek employment elsewhere.

Often we hear someone say, "I am not a slave with a ball and chain but I feel trapped in my job. I cannot get out. I am locked in. I am too old to be hired by some other company and have ten more years before retirement." Or, someone expresses, "I joined the service and my commitment is for four more years. I made a bad decision and feel like a slave. I cannot get out of this."

In such situations, according to Paul, our Lord calls us to do what we do unto Him "knowing that whatever good thing each one does, this he will receive back from the Lord." Nothing is wasted.

Even in marriage some feel bound, but Paul allows for physical separation as I suggested for Sapphira, the wife of Ananias. My mom separated from my dad, due to his rage issues, for five years. She removed herself from this ugly situation. First Corinthians 7:11 sanctions such separation as long as the wife remains unmarried or reconciles.

Submission Prevents Praying against Authorities

Paul wrote in 1 Timothy 2:1–2, "First of all, then, I urge that entreaties and prayers, petitions and thanksgivings, be made on behalf of all men, for kings and all who are in authority, so that we may lead a tranquil and quiet life in all godliness and dignity."

Here Paul is implying that we pray that the authorities do what is of God. Said another way, when authority acts contrary to the heart of Christ, we should not hesitate in asking God to redirect this person entrusted with governance (Proverbs 21:1; Nehemiah 1:11; Ezra 1:1). Submission does not mean we support in prayer every decision an authority makes. Authority can do wrong (Acts 9:14; 26:10). Authority can rob us of leading a tranquil and quiet life in all godliness and dignity.

During the Vietnam War, my friend Jerry Mitchell was an enlisted man who served on a Navy aircraft carrier. What made his tour so extraordinary is that on that ship during that time, God ignited a mini-revival. Many of the crew were Christ-followers and God used them to introduce others to the love of Christ. Many of these crewmen had opportunity to pray with pilots before they launched off the aircraft carrier, some of whom never returned. These pilots welcomed the conversations and prayers. Even so, oddly enough, the chaplain on the ship opposed their efforts. He was liberal to the nth degree, and even had *Playboy* magazines in his office. When he got wind of what these crewmen were doing, he forbid any of their activities. He abused his authority but exercised it nonetheless. This put the men between a rock and a hard place.

Should they obey God or this chaplain? They were not doing anything wrong other than offering to pray with the pilots and others, who appreciated the prayer and discussion about things beyond this life. So, what were they to do?

The men gathered in a storage area to pray about their dilemma with this authoritarian chaplain. They met there often to pray for the pilots and many others desiring God. During that time, Jerry felt strongly to pray that God would stop the chaplain from interfering. To Jerry, this was an abuse of authority and clearly persecution. This was serious since this chaplain had the power and influence to put a halt to their activities. He had oversight over several air craft carriers. In fact, he'd fly from carrier to carrier by helicopter to conduct services. Soon after praying for this chaplain to stop interfering, it so happened the chaplain was returning via helicopter to Jerry's carrier. A gust of wind came out of nowhere, flipped the helicopter upside down in mid-air, and it crashed into the sea. The chaplain was immediately killed but the crew survived. In shock, Jerry and the others gathered in the storage area. They sat in total silence.

Jerry said, "I asked God to stop the chaplain's abuse of power but I did not envision this." Everyone was in awe and humbled by what happened, and felt more strongly than ever that God was doing a gracious work on behalf of the many soldiers who had no guarantees that they'd live past tomorrow. What blessed these men even more is that the new chaplain who replaced the other was a conservative, Bible-believing man of God who fully endorsed all of their activities.

Praying for those in authority means praying the authorities do nothing that contradicts the will of God. God is sovereign and will act according to His wisdom, but He instructs us to pray. Jerry learned that day that God is fully capable of removing bad authorities.

However, submitting to God's will does not eliminate suffering. The Bible says in 2 Timothy 3:12, "all who desire to live godly in Christ Jesus will be persecuted."

Authorities can abuse us. I have always wondered what the early church felt when Herod arrested James and had him beheaded, which then emboldened him to arrest Peter. However, an angel appeared to Peter and miraculously guided him out of the jail (Acts 12:1–9). If the two mothers of James and Peter met, did the mother of James ask the mother of Peter, "Why my boy and not yours?"

From a human perspective, there is no rhyme or reason to the persecution of one and not the other. An evil authority figure like Herod can kill James, but then an angel can counter Herod's abusive authority over Peter. What we know is that God is in charge. Jesus said to Pontius Pilate, "You would have no authority over Me, unless it had been given you from above" (John 19:11). Even so, Pilate had Him crucified. Paul echoes Jesus in Romans 13:1, "For there is no authority except from God, and those which exist are established by God." But the Romans imprisoned Paul for long periods of time and eventually had him beheaded (according to tradition).

Doing God's will does not mean you're going to navigate through a maze that ends up at the spot marked "X" with a treasure to make you rich. Hebrews 11 would tell us otherwise. Dietrich Bonhoeffer himself wrote, "When Christ calls a man, he bids him come and die."[1]

We must recognize praying for or against authority figures is no formula, and more often than not the authority has the power and final say. Herod killed James.

But let's come back to the type of people most of us encounter. We are not dealing with Herods or Hitlers. Such folks do not intend to kill us. However, admittedly, they have ill will toward us. What should we do? Do not hesitate turning to "Jesus Christ our Lord" who has the . . . "dominion and authority, before all time and now and forever" (Jude 25), and therefore can act on behalf of what is right and good, if He so chooses.

Submission Emboldens Bad People

When we submit in doing right because we know it is the right thing to do, it wins praise and silences people who intend to slander us. Read again 1 Peter 2:13–15. It can turn the tables in our favor rather than provide fodder for the critics.

A case in point is David Green, founder of Hobby Lobby. We had the privilege of having a private dinner with David and his wife Barbara. We were in Oklahoma City to speak the next day to his three hundred leaders at Hobby Lobby's headquarters. David shared the story that many months earlier he felt it was right to raise the hourly wage for his employees to fifteen dollars. God had impressed this on his heart. In his opinion, it was the right thing to do. Later this proved to be a wise thing to do. When Hobby Lobby's case came before the US Supreme Court concerning employers being mandated to cover certain contraceptives for female employees, David came under incredible attack by the liberal media. Though that mandate ran contrary to the religious convictions of Hobby Lobby as a company, abortion reflected the fervor and demands of the left. Some in the press set out to politically crucify David Green and Hobby Lobby, and they searched high and low for dirt.

Since liberals had been advocating for a government mandate setting the minimum hourly wage at fifteen dollars, they assumed they could accuse David Green of underpaying his employees, since no other company met that dollar amount. But when they found out he in fact paid his employees fifteen dollars an hour, it stunned these "progressive" critics into utter silence. Even with their irrational animus against Christians, they had nothing bad to say. David had taken the high road and silenced "the ignorance of foolish men" (1 Peter 2:15). Furthermore, he went on to win a landmark decision 5 to 4 on the Court exempting Hobby Lobby's owners from the contraceptive mandate based on their religious beliefs even though they were a for-profit corporation. The organization had so lived consistently with their faith commitment that their objection was not viewed as a ruse. Earlier in the proceedings, at the appellate level, Judge Neil Gorsuch wrote, "All of us must answer for ourselves whether and to what degree we are willing to be involved in the wrongdoing of others." In the case of the plaintiffs, their "faith dictates what is wrongful conduct and their moral culpability in other's acts." He then said, "Some may . . . find the Greens' beliefs offensive. But no one disputes that they are sincerely held religious beliefs . . ."[2]

To the Court, the Greens were sincere people who really wanted to do what was right and avoid what was wrong according to their convictions and conscience. That proved convincing.

We must not lose sight of the power and wisdom of submitting in doing what is right. When we keep doing what is right within our assigned tasks and daily responsibilities, it enhances our credibility and reputation. What bad can anyone say about us? We don't lose influence but gain influence.

Is there an absolute guarantee against slander? Jesus Himself was slandered, and Peter continues in 1 Peter 3:17, "For it is better, if God should will it so, that you suffer for doing what is right rather than for doing what is wrong." Peter also reports that after we do what is right, we can suffer. Authorities can exceed their God-ordained boundaries. They can act unjustly and corruptly. They can lie about us. But in general, doing the right things day in and day out works to our advantage.

Submitting by Righting Our Wrong Is Foolish

When we do wrong, we need to make it right. We need to rebound as fast as we can. Vernon McGee writes, "I have never accepted joyfully a traffic ticket, but I pay my fine and try to be more careful to obey the laws. We are to be obedient to the law because we are giving a testimony."[3] People don't expect us to be perfect but they do expect us to be humble in making right what we did wrong.

What we don't want to do is cover up our wrongdoing with more wrongdoing. Jerry Mitchell also told me of the serviceman on the aircraft carrier that collected new inventory sent to the ship. However, some of what he received had no matching paperwork. Instead of asking about this confusing paperwork and getting clarification from those above him on what he should do, for several months the guy decided to deal with his problem by pushing the equipment overboard. If it wasn't on his sheet to receive, he shoved it off the ship! Hundreds of thousands of dollars of hardware sunk to the bottom of the sea!

Whenever we find ourselves in situations that cause us panic because we don't know what to do, we must guard against doing something wrong as a way of covering our ignorance. For some, this is the default tendency and the consequences down the road when the truth is unearthed exceed the embarrassment we might have felt in coming clean from the get-go. This sailor has to live with why he did not call a time-out and turn to his supervisors with a simple question. "My paperwork shows a problem. I am getting materials that this ship did not request. What should I do with this unrequested inventory?" How hard would it be to ask this question? Doing wrong to save face and cover ignorance will do neither of these.

I know of an office worker who got in over her head with the financial accounting for which she was responsible. Instead of stepping forward and confessing ignorance, she shoved everything in the back of her desk drawers. Out of sight, out of mind. Eventually she was exposed and released of her duties. She lost her job, and finding a similar job elsewhere proved insurmountable; and all of that for jamming papers into the back of her desk drawer because she did not know how to do the accounting. Why not come clean and say, "I am in over my head. I need help"? Immediately righting a wrong saves us from a pattern of wrongs that might never be righted.

None of us are perfect, but we can quickly confess our imperfections. Two wrongs don't make a right. At that moment of failure and humiliation, will we confess, "I don't know the right thing to do"? For certain, we may not know the right thing to do, but we can know it is the right thing to confess we don't know.

When the high priest ordered a soldier to strike Paul across the mouth, Paul said, "God is going to strike you, you whitewashed wall! Do you sit to try me according to the Law, and in violation of the Law order me to be struck?" What spunk! Submission is not a natural impulse even with Paul! However, when bystanders rebuked Paul for going against the law of God, he backed down: "'Do you revile God's high priest?' And Paul said, 'I was not aware, brethren, that he was high priest; for it is written, "You shall not speak evil of a ruler of your people"'" (Acts 23:1–5). When it came to his part of the equation, he confessed it as wrong to make things right.

A Final Thought

As for Peter, he knew a day was coming that Jesus predicted. The authorities would take him where he did not want to go (John 21:19; 2 Peter 1:14). He lived with the realization that an unpleasant death awaited him. I think for this reason he grappled with submission before authorities. We cannot control all of our life, and learning to submit now prepares us for more serious moments, like an unwanted death. As my wife Sarah often shares, "People die the way they lived."

Will you and I be like Jesus who prayed in Luke 23:46, "Father, into Your hands I commit My spirit"? And then "He breathed His last."

Submission isn't all about not getting our way. It is preparing us to transition in deference from this life to the next, and few people think about this.

Chapter 9

GOD'S WILL: ABSTAIN FROM SEXUAL SIN

The next universal will of God is found in 1 Thessalonians 4:3: "For this is the will of God, your sanctification; that is, that you abstain from sexual immorality."

Some have stated, "This chapter will kill the book in light of where many Christians land on abiding by what God reveals in His Word on abstaining from sexual sin." Sadly, many dismiss this teaching by drawing the line of sin just beyond their personal conduct. She moves in with her boyfriend because she loves him and wishes to prove her love to him. He views pornography because everyone does, and besides he isn't actually engaging in the acts. Why does it matter?

Many folks today say, "This Bible stuff about abstaining from sex is ridiculously old-fashioned. God created me as a sexual being to enjoy sex whenever the need arises. He made me this way. I believe He will unfold His unique will no matter what I do sexually. Abstaining from sex is a man-made rule, regressive, and oppressive."

Having said this, I am trusting that there is a generation of believers out there who yearn to experience the unique will of God and are determined to follow this as one of the four universal wills of God. They are serious about

God and their faith. They have no intention to rationalize (Rational Lies) away the treasure of wisdom in Scripture on sexual purity.

These believers recognize that a person who resists this universal will of God deprives themselves of being used of God to the end of his or her life. Sexual activity is between a husband and a wife. These Christ-followers take seriously these kinds of verses:

> Hebrews 13:4: "Marriage is to be held in honor among all, and the marriage bed is to be undefiled; for fornicators and adulterers God will judge."

> 1 Thessalonians 4:3: "For this is the will of God, your sanctification; that is, that you abstain from sexual immorality."

> Hebrews 12:14: "Pursue . . . sanctification without which no one will see the Lord."

> 1 Peter 4:2: "Live the rest of the time in the flesh no longer for the lusts of men, but for the will of God."

> Matthew 5:8: "Blessed are the pure in heart, for they shall see God."

Jesus is clear. The pure in heart see God. Such purity includes sexual purity. It is key to our encounter with the living God.

This line for sexual purity is not difficult to discern, but difficult to obey—which is why some folks aggressively try to change the sexual boundaries to fit their sexual conduct, or why some quit the struggle to abstain from sexual immorality. But, if we desire to know the unique will of God for us, we must begin by following this universal will of God.

Faith and Sex

Does our faith determine our sexual behavior, or does our sexual behavior determine our faith? In his book *Cheap Sex: The Transformation of Men, Marriage, and Monogamy*, University of Texas sociology professor Mark

Regnerus conveys his concern that what ruined Solomon later in his life—sexual relationships with idolatrous, foreign women—is now observed in the church. Faith is eroded as one engages in sexual behaviors that God reveals as hurtful and sinful. Regnerus makes the claim that atheistic science is not killing the faith in young people, but sex outside marriage is. It deadens the religious impulse.[1]

Though young people are looking for companionship and love, when sex comes before marriage, it can adversely affect one's desire to follow Christ. John Stonestreet and G. Shane Morris in an article in *Breakpoint* comment on Regnerus's insights: "Of Americans who regularly attend religious services, 23 percent say they're unsure whether living together outside of marriage is immoral; 21 percent say they don't know what they think of no-strings attached sex. One in four aren't willing to condemn pornography. In fact, that last trend is especially severe. According to Yale sociologist Justin Farrell, evangelicals under thirty are consistently more permissive of pornography than their parents were."[2]

Regnerus found that 90 percent of American young people are engaged in sex. How many of these claim to follow Christ is unknown, but church attendance is dropping off because there is a correlation between sex and faith. Over the years when a person commits adultery, their spouse tells me what the unfaithful partner says during the affair. "I no longer believe in God." This is a standard line I hear repeatedly. When a believer engages in sexual sin, they stop believing (so they say).

How would you answer this question? Is it the lack of faith that causes sex outside of marriage or sex outside of marriage that causes the lack of faith? Most believers know what the Bible teaches on sex and when their behavior doesn't align with the teaching, they stop going to church. They do not move toward the Light. More than we have probably considered, sex leads to a loss of faith.

But what about those who attend church and seek counsel on determining God's will for their life but all the while are sexually active outside of the bonds of marriage?

God's Will before "I Do"

Because I was a pastor in a college town, many dating couples would come in for counseling. They were trying to decide whether or not God was leading them to marry. "Pastor, we really want to know if this relationship is God's will for us. We are really praying about this and want your counsel."

I asked, "Do you really want to know God's will for your relationship?" "Yes, of course, that's why we're here." As I listened to them tell me their story, in the course of the conversation information surfaced that they were living together and sexually active. I then said: "Let me see if I get this straight. You are here today because you want to know God's will for your relationship. Is that right?

"Yes," they agree.

"Yet, 1 Thessalonians 4:3 says, 'For this is the will of God, your sanctification; that is, that you abstain from sexual immorality.' You are not married yet you are having sex. Did you know that God has already revealed His universal will to you for your relationship, but you are disobeying this will?"

At this point, the couple usually looks at each other, wide-eyed and a little sheepish. I continue, "Do you realize that God is not going to reveal His unique will to you on marriage until you obey His universal will on abstaining from sexual immorality? Why? Because if you are disobeying this clear command, guess what? You won't obey if God tells you to end the relationship contrary to your wishes. You are demonstrating that you have no intention to follow God's will when that will counters your desires. Does this question sound too harsh? Please see me as your older brother who cares about you."

Now you can hear a pin drop in the room.

"I wonder," I added in a respectful tone, "if you really do want God's will for your relationship since He has already told you His will, and you have chosen something else. It appears that you are interested in what you want, not what God wants. You are reversing the prayer of Jesus: 'Not Your will be done, but our will be done.' Am I wrong?"

Anyone who has been in love can sympathize with this couple. So why would God ask us to do something that is so hard and feels so unnatural? If God "knows our frame" and understands what we are made of, why would He call us to do something that competes against all the desires He has given us?

Have you ever heard a parent say, "Because I said so"? I suppose we could begin and end this chapter the way some parents answer similar "why-questions" their kids ask. We could simply say, "God says so, so obey." When parents say this, they often hope to protect their kids from ideas they could not possibly understand. Perhaps our heavenly Father is doing the same for us. Paul uses the word *mystery* when referring to the union of a man and a woman and Christ and the church. And, he reminds us in 1 Corinthians 13:12 (NIV), that there are many things we now see "only a reflection as in a mirror; then we shall see face to face." Perhaps the integral role of our spirituality and sexuality is one of them.

Since we live, however, in a culture currently experimenting with and expecting sex outside of marriage and the fallout is becoming clearer over time, I will posit some perspectives on what good God may have intended by asking us to abstain from sexual immorality.

Why does the Bible highlight abstaining from sexual sin as one of the four wills?

For the Married

For the married, the answer is obvious. I remember hearing an old country preacher announce from the pulpit, "When God says 'no,' He means don't hurt yourself!" Ask some celebrities exposed for marital infidelity. Daily news is replete with infidelity by athletes, actors and actresses, politicians, clergy, and other high-profile couples. If you need proof that sexual faithfulness is not an outdated idea, listen to the memoirs of those who were betrayed. Did the spouses of the unfaithful care? You bet they cared!

If we hope to avoid betraying everything we stand for and everyone we love, we must abstain from sexual immorality. Though the secular culture may sanction the unmarried having sex, when it comes to rules for the married, they sing the same old tune: Abstain from sexual immorality or you are in trouble. How can you betray your spouse? The unmet physical or emotional needs that often render one vulnerable to infidelity generally pale in comparison to the deluge of emotional pain unleashed by adultery.

As we listen to stories of the betrayed, one point becomes painfully clear: though our minds have been educated to have a broad view about sex outside marriage, our hearts cannot accommodate the changes. Infidelity still deeply wounds everyone involved, not the least of which are the children. My dad committed adultery; I know.

What If You Have Already Been Unfaithful?

What is God's message to those who have not abstained after marriage? Consider this example of a man in my church whom we will call Rob.

Having committed adultery with a coworker, Rob came to see me when his unfaithfulness to his wife teetered on destroying his family. Though he admitted he loved his wife and children, he was helplessly drawn to the talents of a woman at work. As we discussed his dilemma, he came to realize that the power of Jesus Christ was greater than the forces vying for his heart. Indeed, Christ loved him and died in order to forgive him. Through the crisis and our conversations, Rob placed his faith in Jesus. Immediately thereafter, he knew that he needed to cut off his adulterous relationship. However, he also knew that this woman's presence prohibited him from continuing working with her.

In order to obey Jesus Christ and honor his marriage, Rob quit his job. Because he had an outstanding career, this choice created serious challenges. He had to find new work and wait years to reestablish himself in a new field. There were moments when the cost of obedience seemed overwhelming as he sought to rebuild his life according to God's principles.

At this season of his life, this man resolved to do the universal will of God no matter what the price. Though uncertain of his future and forced to take risks to go forward, Rob stepped out in faith, and God blessed him.

If you give yourself over to God like Rob did, it doesn't mean you're going to get rich. That is not my point. But, if you step out in obedience, God will uniquely bless you as He did Rob. Some of you reading this could experience incredible things if you choose to clean up your sexual life. If you don't obey, this one area of your life will keep shutting down your "Send a Sam" story (see illustration earlier in the book). You will not know God's unique leading until you obey this universal will of God. There are no exceptions.

In the original Greek language of the New Testament, there is no asterisk footnoting your name at the bottom of the parchment saying, "*So-and-so* is the exception to 1 Thessalonians 4:3."

Unmarried but in a Committed Relationship

Some folks who often want to think they are "the exceptions" are those engaged to be married. Their question is: Can we have sex with the person we intend to marry but have not yet married? The Bible uses the word *fornication* to describe this type of sexual relationship and clearly warns against it in a variety of places (Mark 7:21; Acts 15:20; Romans 13:13; Hebrews 13:4). Fornication is sex between unmarried people. Adultery is sex between two people married to someone else. We observe these two concepts in Hebrews 13:4, "Marriage is to be held in honor among all, and the marriage bed is to be undefiled; for fornicators and adulterers God will judge."

Okay, so now the will of God calls us to do something that stands clearly against the mainstream of contemporary practice, especially when it surfaces that some couples who waited to have sex then had horrible marital problems.

So, why would God instruct us to abstain, especially since so many involved in premarital sex applaud the way it enhances intimacy and gives them a chance to find out if they are sexually compatible?

While these reasons appear to make great sense at the outset of the relationship, research does not support that these couples fair any better if they later marry. Indeed, there is considerable evidence from large sample studies collected by the National Survey of Families and Households that suggests those who cohabit before marriage have a far greater incidence of separating and/or divorcing.

Women, for example, who cohabit before marriage are 80 percent more likely to divorce and are almost twice as likely to divorce within ten years as those who do not cohabit. Why? I once spoke to three thousand men and women in France and provided my reason. I said, "A woman moves in with a man to prove to him that she loves him. A man moves in with a woman to determine if he loves her." One could hear the audible gasps of air from the women. That truth struck a chord in the heart of every woman seated there. It is comparable to the chicken and pig walking by an orphanage and the chicken saying to the pig, "Tomorrow, let's provide bacon and eggs for those hungry children." The pig shoots back, "For you, that's a nice gesture. For me, it's total sacrifice." In my opinion, most women totally sacrifice themselves in a relationship only to discover the men they lived with were testing the waters and making nice gestures. Though we all know of exceptions, this may best explain why such high percentages of women quit cohabitating with the man. As they often say, "I realized he never really loved me; not like I loved him. I was all in. He was not."

Equally discouraging is the realization that in a sample of thirteen thousand people who cohabited, at least 40 percent of these couples broke up before marrying. Many of those who did marry reported more dissatisfaction with communication after marrying than those who did not cohabit.[3]

Glenn Stanton in his book, *The Ring Makes All the Difference: The Hidden Consequences of Cohabitation and the Strong Benefits of Marriage*, confirms these findings that a person ignores to their future pain. But what I find intriguing is Glenn's title: *The Ring Makes All the Difference*. Sarah, my wife, strongly conveys at our Love and Respect Marriage Conferences the power of a ring to a woman. Every woman looks at the ring finger of a man and woman. Watch the eyes of a woman when meeting another person for the first time. You will see her glance at the wedding finger, particularly of a female. The ring symbolizes a forever commitment to love and sacrifice for each other.

Research from our Love and Respect Marriage Conferences supports this data. When we surveyed a thousand people who had had premarital sex with the partner they eventually married, we found that the degree of sexual involvement directly correlated with dissatisfaction in communication. The more sexually involved the couple was prior to marriage, the more they now feel:

- disregarded in their views and opinion by their spouse
- judged by their spouse
- controlled by the spouse
- interrupted when talking to their spouse
- dishonesty in the marriage

Likewise, the more sexually involved they were before marriage, the less they feel:

- their spouse makes time for them and cherishes them
- they can calmly discuss something in the marriage
- they can share anything with each other
- they share a deep sense of trust and understanding in the relationship
- they always encourage each other
- they guard themselves from bitterness and anger in the relationship
- they resolve their problems quickly

Why would premarital sex correlate with the above?

I can only speculate, but I suspect that the seeds for future marital problems were planted during habitual premarital sex. For example, I can see why a husband or wife might feel controlled or compromised by the spouse because he or she controlled them sexually before they were married, and they felt compromised. I can also see why dishonesty might be an issue. If they deceived themselves or others about their sexual activity from the get-go, they introduced dishonesty into their marriage. Likewise, if they argued about whether or not to have sex, sex became attached to volatile conversations. Eventually, one or the other might feel judged or insecure about the value of his or her opinion. If they chose to give or withhold sex to appease the other or to assert independence, they compromised their personal integrity and the integrity of the relationship.

For Christian couples who know that premarital sex hurts God's heart, the real struggle is with guilt. The pleasure of their sexual involvement is continually attacked by the realization that sexual appetites dominate their decisions. Indeed, it overrides their desire to obey God. Over time, the habit of using sex to silence other important conversations eventually erodes their personal sense of peace, as well as peace in the relationship. Having opted for rationalizing their wrongdoing in favor of short-term solutions, the couple develops habits of burying pain rather than confronting it and resolving it.

Most importantly, couples engaged in premarital sex forfeit the opportunity to really communicate with each other on other levels. If private time revolves around sexual activity, then spending time cherishing the heart of each other falls by the wayside. When God says "no," He means, "Don't hurt yourself." Sadly, some don't get this simple point: disobey God's universal will and forfeit the experience of His unique will!

Living Together

I heard a man at Northwoods Church in Peoria, Illinois, share about a time that all hell broke loose in his life. One thing after another set him back: loss of job, an arrest, debt, etc. He never connected his problems with living with his girlfriend. It was only after a pastor questioned his sexual purity that he understood the correlation. When he then separated from her so that they could walk in moral purity, his hellish nightmares subsided. He testified to the truth of God's Word: "Marriage is to be held in honor among all, and the marriage bed is to be undefiled; for fornicators and adulterers God will judge" (Hebrews 13:4).

He truly believed he was under God's loving discipline, which is the meaning of God's discipline, which the writer of Hebrews had just explained in chapter 12. Though God accepted him unconditionally, He refused to let him grieve and quench the Holy Spirit via sexual impurity. God had a call on his life, and his impurity prevented him from God's best.

This does not mean that everyone stressed by a job loss, an arrest, and debt is under God's discipline, only that this man knew this about himself. That's why each of us needs to stop to consider if we are under the loving disciplinary action of God precisely because of our sexual immorality. None of us must be so foolish as to conclude that a loving God could not care less about our sexual activities and appetites. He cares deeply, which is why in love He disciplines or judges fornicators and adulterers. That sounds cruel to some but they refuse to believe God loves us and knows what is best for us. Furthermore, they refuse to believe God is hurt by us. Yes, you heard that correctly. Ezekiel reported what God felt when he penned, "I have been hurt by their adulterous hearts which turned away from Me" (6:9). Do we really believe we hurt God's heart? God is not some cosmic killjoy but our loving heavenly Father, and what we do on the sexual front affects Him.

Though the world argues that cohabitation allows two people to gain confidence in the rightness of the relationship, God's Word never changes. By way of analogy, the captain of a battleship moving forward full throttle can demand that the ensign in the lighthouse cease telling him, the captain of a mighty warship, to change course. But the lighthouse is a permanent fixture on land, so the captain had better heed the advice about changing course, not vice versa. The lighthouse is immutable. God the Father's permanent standard on sexual purity pulsates in Scripture. It is a dominant theme, not a marginal issue, and is one of the four wills. And, there is no evidence biblically that God has changed His mind. I remember hearing years ago, "God makes the rules, Emerson, not you." It is irreverent and reckless for us to declare that He should change His position or that He has no position on sexual behavior.

Sadly, some of us have never connected the dots on God's discipline of us as this fellow in Peoria finally did.

Why? Jeremiah declared, "The heart is more deceitful than all else and is desperately sick; who can understand it?" (Jeremiah 17:9). Though we can have good desires on many fronts, like giving to the poor and doing pro bono work, or even caring altruistically for the person with whom we have sex, when we habitually sin in the sexual realm, and lie to ourselves about this sin, we are committing a flagrant foul. God then ejects us from His game plan for us. Though we are still on His team with His uniform on, we are out of the game. We forfeit His personal coaching, so to speak. We will watch from the bench while others make great gains. Couples who live together cannot escape His discipline. Hebrews 12 reminds us that God loves us too much to be indifferent.

But, you may ask, if sexual purity is God's will, why must we struggle and feel so bad in the face of our weaknesses? And, why must we subject ourselves to the mocking of the world? C. S. Lewis wrote:

> No man knows how bad he is till he has tried very hard to be good. A silly idea is current that good people do not know what temptation means. This is an obvious lie. Only those who try to resist temptation know how strong it is. After all, you find out the strength of the German Army by fighting it, not by giving in. You find out the strength of the wind by trying to walk against it, not by lying down. A man who gives in to temptation after five minutes simply does not know what it would have been like an hour later. That is why bad people, in one sense, know very little about badness. They have lived a sheltered life by always giving in. We never find out the strength of the evil impulse inside us until we try to fight it: and Christ, because He was the only man who never yielded

to temptation, He is the only man who knows to the full what temptation means—the only complete realist.[4]

Single and Choosing Celibacy

Are you single and tired of struggling to remain sexually pure? You have a Savior who understands. Jesus Himself lived thirty-three years as a celibate man. Though He enjoyed the company of close female friends and followers, He lived, worked, and traveled without the intimacy of a sexual relationship. The many believers who find themselves in the singles' world for a long season of adult life have this hope: their Savior knows their plight. He has walked in their shoes. The challenge to stay sexually pure, unfortunately, confronts singles on multiple levels. Long hours alone create hunger for recreation, companionship, affirmation, compassion, and intimacy. Since the secular social networks seem to revolve around two separate nuclei—the family or the swinging singles group—Christians who are committed to sexual purity often find themselves the odd man (or woman) out. When work ends on Friday night, they aren't looking for "hookups" at the single's bar, but they do long for something besides another night alone. As they wait in expectation for God's choice of a mate for them, the loneliness and temptations can be overwhelming.

I do not know if the early disciples ever imagined a world with so many adult singles living outside the context of families when they stressed the importance of abstaining from fornication. I do know that some of the singles who were apostles or followers of Christ used their time as singles to make a huge impact on the world. Paul, Timothy, and John are a few of the prominent examples. Their ability to abandon themselves to the service of Christ in their own communities and around the world is the reason the good news of Christ spread so quickly. God ordains marriage. He also extols the unique gift of singlehood as Paul notes in 1 Corinthians 7. Listen to the way Eugene Peterson describes this in his contemporary version of 1 Corinthians 7:32–35 (The Message):

> I want you to live as free of complications as possible. When you're unmarried, you're free to concentrate on simply pleasing the Master. Marriage involves you in all the nuts and bolts

of domestic life and in wanting to please your spouse, leading to so many more demands on your attention. The time and energy that married people spend on caring for and nurturing each other, the unmarried can spend in becoming whole and holy instruments of God. I'm trying to be helpful and make it as easy as possible for you, not make things harder. All I want is for you to be able to develop a way of life in which you can spend plenty of time together with the Master without a lot of distractions.

Many singles today, however, grow weary of constant sexual temptation and succumb to sex outside marriage. They buy the lies of our culture about its "rightness." Or, they simply get tired of waiting for a spouse and decide not to "miss out on a good thing." Others have never really been given a good enough reason to abstain.

As my daughter, Joy, says:

Abstaining is so difficult to tackle because while it simply can be, "Don't have sex outside of marriage," our sexuality is so much more complicated than that. What does God mean when He tells us to abstain? Why does He tell us to abstain? Will He really hold true to 1 Corinthians 10:13 (ESV), which promises: "No temptation has overtaken you that is not common to man. God is faithful, and he will not let you be tempted beyond your ability, but with the temptation he will also provide the way of escape, that you may be able to endure it"?

Really? Will He? Because this is hard. I am pretty sure I wasn't given the gift of celibacy. So I have to figure out what celibacy is for me. For a long time I was pretty sure it just meant, don't have sex, but everything else is a go. I never took the time to figure out why God had given these instructions.

So why is abstaining from sexual immorality so important for singles? Given the emotional and social issues compounding the absence of physical pleasure, why expect anyone to postpone sexual involvement until marriage? Before birth control pills, one could argue that abstaining from sex outside marriage prevented the consequences of unplanned pregnancies. What about now? Are there good reasons to avoid premarital sex beyond the possible transmission of STDs?

This is a complex topic, one that is well beyond the purpose of this book, but let me offer a few ideas from recent research on human sexuality. In a book entitled *Hooked: The Bonding Power of Sex*, authors Dr. Freda Bush and Dr. Joe McIlhaney examine the neurophysiology of sex and its consequent ability to create long lasting emotional bonds. They contend that several chemical responses accompanying sex foster both hunger for repetition and deep emotional bonding—two attributes which were intended to work for the pleasure and productivity of a married couple. The "high" triggered by the release of dopamine during intercourse creates desire for repetition. The increase of receptors for oxytocin in females and vasopressin in males promotes feelings of attachment. "So," as Drs. Bush and McIlhaney purport, "those in a relationship not only have the dopamine that rewards them for the repeating of the act, but also the oxytocin and the vasopressin that makes them feel attached. Thus, we have the name of our book *Hooked*. You become attached, addicted, bonded to each other."[5]

Such intense attachment following sex is nature's way of providing a bond for couples to stay together. According to the authors, the abuse of sexuality that occurs through casual sex with multiple partners disrupts this process and often leads to severe emotional concerns. Without commitment, one may simply become addicted to "newness" with a variety of partners or hopelessly emotionally attached to a casual sexual partner who is not interested in developing a long-term relationship.

The Creator's View

As sexual experimentation outside marriage continues, there may be more evidence to support the position that God, our Creator, has already ordained: abstinence is for our good. Indeed, God feels so strongly about the importance of abstaining outside marriage that He stresses the dire consequences in a variety of verses. According to Mark 7:20–23, sexual immorality has the power to defile the whole man. Because of this, 1 Corinthians 6:9 warns that fornicators will not inherit the kingdom of God. Hebrews 13:4

confirms this by stating that God disciplines sexual immorality: "Marriage is to be held in honor among all, and the marriage bed is to be undefiled; for fornicators and adulterers God will judge."

Since the consequences of sexual sin are so great, Paul cautions believers to "Flee immorality. Every other sin that a man commits is outside the body, but the immoral man sins against his own body" (1 Corinthians 6:18).

Tough? Yes. Uncompromising? You bet. Counterculture? Absolutely. The Bible addresses this topic in a straightforward fashion with clear warning because sexual immorality defiles the inner man, waging war against the soul and incurring the discipline of God. Arguing that premarital sex, adultery, or sexual immorality is no big deal does not hold up to Scripture or most social research. Yet, many couples, instead of taking steps to guard their hearts out of love for God, rationalize their sexual relationship and move forward as though their love for each other sanctions it.

Is this a one-sided deal? Does God have all the say and we have all the responsibility? When God commands, He rewards obedience. This command comes from the heart of a loving God which when we obey from our heart, we unleash His kindness in directing our steps in unique and personal ways. The upside is beyond words.

When our heavenly Father tells us no, He is not only preventing us from experiencing harm, His intent is to open new doors to us that bring us joy as He unfolds a special leading which we have activated from our obedience.

Chapter 10
SEXUAL TEMPTATIONS

Not Guilty?

If you have made it this far into our look at the topic of sexual immorality and you are still able to plead, "Not Guilty," you can praise God for the strength of His protection and your self-control.

By the way, a person who can control their sexual appetites often can control every area of their life, so this is no small matter. This may be one of the reasons that God highlights abstaining from sex outside marriage. The Lord knows if you get this area under control, He can trust you in the face of most temptations.

But here is the real deal: Jesus wants your whole heart and mind. Though the Mosaic Law warns against adultery, when Jesus came, He "raised the bar," so to speak. Now, the law is not solely, "Do not commit adultery"; but rather, as Jesus explains, "Anyone who looks at a woman lustfully has already committed adultery with her in his heart" (Matthew 5:27–28 NIV). Adultery is not just a "hands-on" experience, but a "what's in your head?" and "where's your heart?" experience. How many can plead, "Not Guilty"?

In the next few pages, I am going to challenge you to consider two areas of modern life that excite "lust" and tend to lead people to commit adultery in the heart. These areas involve the lure of images and ideas in pornography and romance novels. While neither of these pursuits involves a true physical adultery, their pull on our passions through our fantasies has a similar effect on our hearts. And, as we've noted, adultery "in his [her] heart" is the concern of our Lord.

Please keep in mind your experience of God's blessing and power on your personal life as you commit to purity. Jesus said that the pure in heart will see God (Matthew 5:8). Allow your heart to engage what Jesus reveals. Good things await you in your encounter with the unique will of God for your life.

Pornography

How important is avoiding pornography to receiving God's blessing?

We need a clear definition of what pornography is and a broader inclusion of other pitfalls men (and women) will face with pornography, both now and in the future, as technology and culture change.

The dictionary says that pornography is "printed or visual material containing the explicit description or display of sexual organs or activity, intended to stimulate erotic rather than aesthetic or emotional feelings" (Google Dictionary).

If that definition causes you to wonder where the line is for you, then subscribe to the famous phrase, "I know it when I see it." This was the phrase used in 1964 by United States Supreme Court Justice Potter Stewart in describing hard core pornography. Though there is a subjective element in this evaluation, the Justice was onto something.

Actually, this need not be tough to define for ourselves. We are not creating a definition for others. For the Christ-follower, the phrase should be, "I know it when I see it because it excites an element of lust in me." James writes, "But each one is tempted when he is carried away and enticed by his own lust. Then when lust has conceived, it gives birth to sin; and when sin is accomplished, it brings forth death" (James 1:14–15). In other words, on an individual basis each of us must know the threshold of "his own lust." This isn't about arguing with someone else about the definition of pornography but about knowing what is pornographic to ourselves.

Of course, this demands that we be totally honest about our own sexual temperament and vulnerabilities. What I have found is that we tend to lie to ourselves about our sophisticated capacity to engage sexual content without lust. I have concluded about myself, I am more vulnerable than I wish to admit; and the Holy Spirit is more conservative when whispering in my ear than I wish Him to be.

This isn't stated to become legalistic. This isn't so much about avoiding pornography but keeping our focus on experiencing the unique leading of God in our lives and removing anything that quenches Him from moving. I like to say, "Stop thinking of the number nine, and when you do, raise your hand." Of course, everyone now thinks of the number nine until finally one soul raises their hand. I ask how they stopped thinking of the number nine. They said, "I thought of the number five." That applies here. We must not think about stopping everything related to pornography or it will stay in front of us. Instead, we need to catch a vision for what God will do uniquely in and through us as we follow His four wills.

Let me add, we live in the world and cannot always help the first sight or reading. It really comes down to the continuation of looking and reading. Martin Luther said, "You cannot keep birds from flying over your head, but you can keep them from building a nest in your hair."

Pornography Everywhere

Due to rapid technological advances that have led to breakneck cultural change, the American culture has been pornified to such an extent that men (and women) engage in pornographic entertainment in places not previously experienced. I believe that in the beginning of the age of Internet pornography, it was limited to "porn websites," where explicit videos were posted, and so on. Now, it is embedded in almost all TV shows, films, social media sites, novels, and so on, so that porn will come and find *you*. Even when a person is not "addicted" to porn websites, exposure has mushroomed. Many people are no longer avoiding sexual temptation by virtue of their supposed tolerance of this form of entertainment on a yearly basis.

Yes, we are bombarded and it only takes a little exposure here and there on a regular basis to distract us in our walk with Christ and ignite the lust within. But do we wish to admit such vulnerability and that the Holy Spirit is leading us to be more Christ-focused?

Each of us must know what is going on in our inner person and make a decision to do what we know is best for our relationship to God. The pure in heart see God, Jesus said. Where our "own lust" is ignited on a regular basis (a nest is forming), we need to take steps to keep ourselves free so God will actively move in our lives. Such steps are liberating. We are not entering a prison yard with barbed wired fence, but putting up a guardrail to prevent us from driving off a cliff.

A pastor of a megachurch came to the podium after hearing this message on the four wills and told his congregation: "I know the day and hour I said 'no' to pornography." He claims this decision catapulted him into the sphere of God's personal leading of his life. Obeying this universal will opened doors for his life and ministry. Every man comes to the same crossroad. Which way will he go? Is this a harmless thing since he really isn't doing the actual act of sex?

Listen to the other side of the story of pornography. A wife writes, "My husband of nearly thirty-three years is addicted to porn and has been since age eighteen. He claims to be a Christian but will not deal with this addiction or make any attempt to get counseling. He told me he stopped, but today I found out he is still going to Internet sites with porn. I feel sick to my stomach right now and don't know what to do . . . I feel like he has been committing adultery for all our married life." This man is forfeiting God's almighty power in his life and harming the heart of his wife.

Another wife wrote: "What I discovered is that my husband has had an ongoing problem with pornography . . . he told me I was over-reacting—it was no big deal—everyone does it. Then in February of this year, I discovered that he has been spending enormous amounts of time on the Internet, and the sites he was accessing were of pre-teens and pre-adolescent girls . . . When I confronted him, he told me he has done nothing wrong . . . he feels that I am the problem in the marriage. I don't believe this is my fault. He is a grown man, able to make his own decisions."

This man's denial of responsibility clearly prohibits the moving of God in his soul. His denial of fact ("The porno viewing never happened"), his denial of the seriousness of the sin ("Porn is no big deal"), and his denial of personal responsibility ("I'm not to blame, you are") reveal his true denial of God and his enslavement to his habit. If this man remains entrapped, he will forfeit experiencing the unique will of God in his life. There are no two ways about this.

Contrast this man's denial of his habit with the testimony of the following man we will call Jim, who came to terms with the addictive effect of pornography in his life:

> I was totally addicted to porn. There were times when I spent nearly the whole day at work looking at porn . . . I would leave for work early and come home late in order to do porn. I spent thousands of dollars on Internet porn and made up lies to my wife about the charges on our credit card . . . I felt so guilty for what I had done. By now, we had three precious children. My wife was more sweet and beautiful than ever to me and had done a wonderful job at maintaining a shapely figure. I can remember so well how sick I would feel . . . "Why am I doing this? My own wife looks so much better to me than these women." Sometimes, I became so sick, I would literally retch. I continually begged God to forgive and deliver me.

God did answer Jim's prayer for release; but not until he confessed and disclosed his sinful practices (James 5:16; Acts 19:18). When a sin is brought into the light before people who can help, the grip of the darkness subsides before the light of Christ. Accountability matters: bad behaviors change when others are watching.

Jim continues, "Finally after five years of porn, God put me under such extreme conviction that I was willing to do whatever it took to really be delivered. I started by confessing (to another) . . . Immediately, when I confessed . . . God came so sweetly to my heart and removed the root of sin. This happened over six months ago. I have not gone back . . ." Wow! Upon confession to another, he encountered the unique presence of God as he obeyed God's will to abstain from sexual immorality.

Jim's life has been totally transformed since the moment of his confession. Wanting to "share how faithful God has been in [his] struggle with pornography," he began a workshop for men at his church. Most of the attendees, he now rejoices, "are reporting back with very positive testimonies, and we can see the changes occurring in their marriages. Men are getting into accountability relationships and talking!"

The sphere of Jim's influence for God continues to enlarge. When he shared his testimony from the pulpit, he was surprised that, "dozens of women came up to me and thanked me for sharing." He rejoices that "God is even using my weakness to provide evangelistic opportunities." Since Jim's company administers the computer network for the city, and he now has the job of auditing Internet usage, he was able to discover and report some inappropriate activity to the city director. "The circumstances and timing were so God," he says. "It allowed me to share my testimony, share Jesus as the key, and open a 'godly' dialogue with key individuals in local government and the local police force, something I've been praying about for years. God is so faithful." Jim obeyed the universal will of God and then experienced God's unique will for him.

When it comes to sexual immorality and addictions, you must do as Jim did—"whatever it takes"—to obey God. And, you cannot do it alone. I love Alcoholics Anonymous because they shrewdly get this. At the beginning of every meeting, they greet each other. "Hi, I'm Joe. I'm an alcoholic who has not drunk for fourteen years." They never stop identifying themselves as alcoholics. A recovering alcoholic no longer argues he is free to go to a bar. This addiction is bigger than he is, and he accepts this. Once an alcoholic, always an alcoholic—who happens to no longer drink. Instead of denying the addiction, he develops a lifestyle around it. He stays out of bars. He can't win in there. The same applies to an addiction to pornography or any sexual immorality. Each one of us must admit that we have sexual impulses that overpower us in certain settings. In many instances, childhood sexual experiences set off chemical reactions in the brain that are deep-seated. Instead of denying this control, the only way through it is to agree that we have something innate, carnal, and permanent within that influences us, and will always influence us. The apostle Paul warns us against telling ourselves that we have this thing beat. He writes, "let him who thinks he stands take heed that he does not fall" (1 Corinthians 10:12). Each day we must recognize that today we may fall into sexual temptation and must take steps to prevent it. Acknowledging this enslavement leads to personal freedom.

Romance Novels

Some women also struggle with an addiction to pornography. Even in the days of Ezekiel, there were women who "saw men portrayed on the wall, images of the Chaldeans portrayed with vermilion, girded with belts on their loins, with flowing turbans on their heads, all of them looking like officers. . . . When she saw them she lusted after them . . ." (Ezekiel 23:14–16). Yes, some women idolize men's bodies.

Many more, however, struggle with sexual and emotional fantasies offered through romance novels, and we can add romance movies. Is reading a romance novel just a harmless pasttime or is something else at stake here? Consider for a moment the following woman's response to reading romance novels. She explains her passion for them this way:

> While I was reading, I was completely "in" the story, and I could "feel'" what the female character felt. . . . The best part . . . of the book is reading just how absolutely in love the characters are. The way she sees him, as the most beautiful and perfect being in the whole world . . . and the way she melts and hyperventilates when he looks into her eyes. It's the best because I can "escape" into this fantasy world and "pretend" that I'm her for the time being. I would be lying if I said I didn't want to see and feel for someone the way she does him, almost as if nothing he does or says or is could ever be wrong. He's just that perfect (at least to me).[1]

What is going on here? Is this woman's appetite for romance with the "perfect" man a healthy outlet for her need for emotional intimacy? *Pornia* (the Greek word for sexual immorality) includes, in a metaphorical or figurative sense, the idea that someone draws another away into idolatry, including the idolatry of romance.[2]

Might we call the above woman's pursuit of the "perfect" man a modern version of the idolatry of romance similar to the ancient worship of Aphrodite, the goddess of romance? And, if so, is this a problem?

I know a single woman who ministered on a major college campus. She personally led sixty women to Jesus Christ in one year. As an evangelist and disciple, she was incredible. Later, she married a godly, wise man, and for a ten-year period they mentored ninety individuals who went into full-time ministry because of them. Few couples have had such a phenomenal influence. But prior to the marriage, this godly woman called off the wedding two times. She was drawn to the character in *Funny Girl* starring Barbara Streisand, not unlike the girl who read the romance novel. Though this woman was not taken with the male lead per se, she did desire to live the fantasized life of the woman captured on the silver screen, which is why we must add romance movies to romantic novels. Fortunately a wise person challenged her: "Are you into real love or reel love?" She snapped out of her deception. Godly-wise folks need to realize that Hollywood can impact us more than God's Holy Word.

Dare I suggest that her romantic and sensual fantasy for the "perfect" mate equals a man's sexual fantasy for the perfect playmate? I am suggesting we consider the similarities in motivation and effect. The "perfect" male in romantic prose speaks to the female, "I am here for you, to meet your needs, love you, and be intimate with you." In much the same way, a seductive woman in a sexual pose speaks to the male, "I am here for you, to meet your needs, admire you, and be intimate with you." Both seek satisfaction of their deep need for love and respect.

Am I downplaying a husband's addiction to porn and shaming a wife who reads romance novels? No, I am trying to show that both men and women need to be honest about their gender longings that can displease the Lord. Just because a woman does not lust the same way a man does, does not mean the Lord will not hold her accountable for her carnal desires. A woman can "feel sensual desires in disregard of Christ" (1 Timothy 5:11). She can listen to the words of people who "entice by fleshly desires, by sensuality" (2 Peter 2:18). Though sexual images may have little impact on her, if she dreams about someone who is not her husband, she is hardly reverencing the Lord who loves her. Again, we must be totally honest with ourselves about romance novels and movies. "Am I more vulnerable than I wish to admit, and is the Holy Spirit more Christ-focused when whispering in my ear than I wish Him to be?" The mind-set upon the things of the flesh runs counter to the mind-set upon the things of the Holy Spirit (Romans 8:5–9).

A person who listened to our Love and Respect podcasts wrote,

Lately the Lord has been breaking me from a long-held stronghold. I would even call it an idol. From an early age, I loved fairy tales: the concept of beautiful princesses in towers rescued by knights in shining armor. As I grew older, that continued to be a part of my personality. I loved reading romantic stories, fantasizing about my future husband, etc. Intrinsically, this interest in romance is innocent and can even reflect our desire for Jesus. However, I did not pursue it in a way that was God-honoring or spiritual. Instead, it became an unhealthy and sinful obsession in my teenage and young adult years. Though I began by reading Christian romance novels, I (sadly) graduated into more and more graphic romance novels and eventually, and much to my shame, pornography.

Upon my marriage, the majority of those unhealthy (and downright sinful) actions were put away, only to start creeping up as I began a disturbing trend of measuring my husband by my pre-married concepts of a "knight in shining armor." Looking back, I can see how this slippery slope happened, and it began with me neglecting my time with the Lord. Soon, in my heart I was questioning whether my husband was right for me, if he could really satisfy me, if he really loved me, if there was someone "better" for me out there, etc., etc. Finally, the Lord brought me to my senses and pointed out this incredibly dangerous downward spiral. I began speaking truth over myself, singing praise songs, renewing my time in Scripture, and removing temptations from my life.

I do not consider myself "done" with this journey. I am sure I will need to refocus my attention off this unhealthy idol many times. I must train myself in godliness instead. I don't know where it comes from, which bothers me greatly. If it ever started out as a good desire, it has been corrupted by my sin nature. The heart is truly deceptive above all else!

My heart goes out to her and many in this situation, if for no other reason no one is pointing out how deceptive this is for women in particular. We would all be shocked if in the Christian book stores we had signs saying,

"Christian porn for men over here, mainly pictures. Christian porn for women over here, mainly words." Or, would we? Would we only be appalled at having something for men? Would we argue that we are wrongly shaming women? "All women want is to love. All men want is to lust!"

Eve's Deception (Genesis 3:7)

Sarah and I recently sat with a godly and good-willed man who ministers for Christ. Since we have known him well for three decades, we grieved to learn his wife had threatened a couple of times to leave him. As he sat before us weeping over his marriage, Sarah asked, "Is your wife reading romance novels?" I never thought to ask this because of his wife's godliness. He replied immediately, "Oh, yes, all the time. She tells me that she gets her relational needs met through Christian romance novels." Like Eve, this wife was deceived into thinking she was being deprived of a harmless "good"—in this case, romantic love (1 Timothy 2:13). To enliven herself, she satisfied her longings for affection by reading about a man romantically pursuing a woman. Because the novels met her deep emotional needs and brought her "delight" and "wise" insight into what an ideal marriage ought to be, she concluded that the novels were "good" for her. But, the novels only fostered dissatisfaction with her spouse. Soon this woman was looking around for couples enjoying romance. She watched them walk hand in hand in the parks and eat by candlelight at restaurants. To her, these unknown couples had found their soul mates. One day she decided to flirt with a man at work.

Is this an unusual scenario? Unfortunately, not at all.

The Same Root: Enslavement

While unmet emotional needs drive many women to fantasize about other men, even fictional men, do these feelings justify fantasy or affairs? Many women who commit adultery rationalize that their need for love justifies their actions. They contend that their need for love is not lust. But does this parallel Eve's deception? Most men know their lust problem is sin when having sexual desires for another woman. It is black and white. Whereas most women find themselves dreaming of love, albeit with another man, and that is not viewed as lustful nor sinful because it does not feel dark or shameful. But Eve was deceived and seduced by what felt good and delightful, not dark and demonic, though the demons were behind it. After all, a "lust for love" is good and a man's "love of lust" is evil. Maybe this is why Proverbs 30:20, says: "This is the way of an adulterous woman: She eats and wipes her mouth, and says, 'I have done no wrong.'" Her need for love warps her perspective. "Love," she concludes, "is 'good.' It's a 'delight' that makes me 'wise.' There is nothing wrong here."

Some women argue that reading novels and fantasizing is a lot less harmful than looking for a real-life person to meet these needs. But, the question is: What effect does reading a romantic novel have on the heart of the reader and the spouse? One husband wrote, "My wife has been reading fiction since we were married—Christian and secular fiction. I picked them up a few times and looked them through. A few steamy parts here and there, but I thought they were harmless for a woman. Now I hate them. At least the last time I looked at a naked centerfold I knew it was a fantasy, and I would have to sell my job and family to have one. I don't think some women see anything wrong with these novels."

Most women, I suspect, would have a hard time equating their obsession with romance novels to a man's absorption with pornography; but the effect on their hearts and the heart of their spouse may be the same. As this man says, "I never heard a pastor say 'I want everyone in the congregation to bring *Playboys* and *Harlequins* to the burn barrel tonight.' No, it's always just the *Playboys*. What the heck is wrong with people?" he adds. "I would never hold up a *Playboy* to my wife and say 'You need to look like that.' I'd be stupid. So why do women have no problem holding up all these fantasies to a man?'"

Am I calling all romance writing sinful? Not if we keep the Song of Solomon in the Bible. Neither am I calling all books on sexual intimacy sinful. I am only saying that this fantasy can quench and grieve the Holy Spirit equal to a male's pornographic fantasy. Both are forms of idolatry because both put worship of an ideal above the act of loving a real other. Both, in essence, are forms of self-indulgence. The difference is that most men know their behavior is sinful, while many women justify fantasy because it feels "good . . . delightful . . . wise." Adam knew he disobeyed. Eve did not know she was deceived.

Those who are trying to escape their hunger for relational intimacy through the fantasies of pornography or romance novels are plagued by the same root problem—enslavement.

Peter reminds us in 2 Peter 2:19, whatever controls us enslaves us: "For by what a man is overcome, by this he is enslaved." In other words, if we are continually allowing ourselves to be overcome by sexual immorality, we will be addicted. When we keep pursuing sexual relationships, viewing pornography, or indulging in fantasies, we will bring pain to our personal lives. In 2 Peter 2:19, Peter decries the damage done by those with "eyes full of adultery" (v. 14): "They promise freedom to everyone. But they are merely slaves of filthy living because people are slaves of whatever controls them" (CEV). Though our culture promises you freedom related to these things and promotes them as healthy, Jesus said, "I tell you most solemnly that anyone who chooses a life of sin is trapped in a dead-end life and is, in fact, a slave" (John 8:34 MSG).

No Longer Enslaved

Is this what you want? Do you think you'll be an exception? It's not likely. The profits from porn and romance novels as well as the statistics on those having sex outside of marriage reveal that many are losing the battle to stay pure. The end for all is some kind of enslavement—sexual, emotional, or mental.

Of all the reasons for avoiding sex outside of marriage, this may be the most important. Anything that absorbs our passions controls us and redirects our focus from God. This is likely the reason that Paul puts the command to avoid sexual immorality right after the command to be sanctified: "For this is the will of God, your sanctification; that is, abstain from sexual immorality" (1 Thessalonians 4:3).

What God really wills, as you can see, is our sanctification. Since sanctification means being "set apart for holy purposes," we can deduce that Paul considers sex outside of marriage a primary barrier to being used by God for His holy purposes. As Peter says, "Just as he who called you is holy, so be holy in all you do; for it is written: Be holy, because I am holy" (1 Peter 1:15–16 NIV, original reference Leviticus 11:44–45).

Anything that dominates you so that your focus strays from God prevents you from being set apart for His holy purposes. But, when you abstain from sexual immorality and are filled with God's Spirit, you are free to experience the kind of fruit that comes from living a holy and sanctified life:

- *peace* and *joy* deep in the heart because you know God's love
- *confidence* in worship and prayer because you have a clean conscience
- *meaningful study* of the Word that leads to personal applications
- *authentic fellowship* with other believers
- *spiritual authority*, *credibility*, and *influence* in ministry as others observe the life you lead

What If We Fail?

Does your heart hunger for these things? Many of you are experiencing them already because you have set yourselves apart for God, to walk as He walked and to do the work He intends for you to do. You are living the sanctified life, even if at times the price seems high. Please have confidence in God when you ask Him to direct your steps.

Many of those I have pastored commit to abstain and yet still fall short. They admit to wanting to live in sexual purity, but feel defeated by persistent failures. They ask: What do we do if we fail—again and again? I have always liked C. S. Lewis's depiction of God's response to the predicament of ongoing human failure. He says:

> No amount of falls will really undo us if we keep on picking ourselves up each time. We shall be very muddy and tattered children by the time we reach home. But the bathrooms are all ready, the towels put out, and clean clothes in the airing cupboard. The only fatal thing is to lose one's temper and give it up. It is when we notice the dirt that God is most present in us; it is the very sign of His presence.[3]

We must not let defeat defeat us. We must get back up and once again seek God's forgiveness.

When I was a new believer, I heard professor and scholar Dr. Gordon Fee tell the story of Christ's forgiveness of a repentant believer. When this believer came before the Lord to confess his sin, he said humbly, "Lord Jesus,

I have sinned again. Will You forgive me again?" The Lord replied, "Again? I don't recall the last time."

I wept at that story. I could not comprehend the wonder of God's love and forgiveness. Though Dr. Fee was not talking only about sexual sin, but sin in general, I rejoiced at the reality that I could start again. The type of sin does not matter. If sexual sin is your battle, you can begin again! The gift of forgiveness applies to every sin. You must start again. Not from presumption, but from gratefulness and brokenness. Knowing this motivates us to fight the fight and to win.

Do you need to start again in this area of your life? Have your sexual behaviors or fantasies blocked the power of God's work in your life?

Remember, the Bible says, "No temptation has overtaken you that is not common to man. God is faithful, and he will not let you be tempted beyond your ability, but with the temptation, he will also provide the way of escape, that you may be able to endure it" (1 Corinthians 10:13 ESV). Jesus tells us "the spirit indeed is willing, but the flesh is weak." But, if we "watch and pray" we will "not enter into temptation" (Mark 14:38 ESV). We need to pray, "Lord, I feel so weak. Strengthen me. I feel so helpless. Help me. I feel so cornered. Show me the exit. I feel so pulled. Pull me back."

We need to invite others to pray for us in the same way. In so doing, we are telling a godly, wise person of our temptations. That is important because bringing ourselves into the light sets in motion this axiom: observed behavior changes. When we bring our vulnerabilities into the light for others to see, the stranglehold on us often lessens because watching eyes motivate us to do the right thing. We can "stimulate" and "sharpen" each other and even be healed by such transparent confession (Hebrews 10:24; Proverbs 27:17; James 5:16).

The Promise of a "Hope and a Future"

The Lord longs to answer your prayers, uniquely leading you, but you need to discern that if your sexual and sensual appetites are controlling you, then you are standing in the path of the personal and powerful leading of God in your life. If you are disobeying this universal will of God, forget asking God to direct your steps uniquely. If, however, you move forward by committing to control yourself and believing God will provide a way of escape, you can expect that God will honor you.

Even in the worst of times for the nation of Israel, God promised Jeremiah, "'For I know the plans I have for you,' declares the Lord, 'plans to prosper you and not to harm you, plans to give you hope and a future'" (Jeremiah 29:11 NIV). God also longs to offer you a "hope and a future," especially in this important area of intimacy and sexuality.

Chapter 11
DOES IT WORK?

How did the four wills work in my life? Perhaps my personal story can encourage you. But do know, I am still on the journey with you and must revisit this checklist of the four wills on a regular basis. Truly, these four greatly encourage and challenge me. For all the reasons stated in this book, they just make sense. They guide and guard me. God uses them to direct my steps and to free me to direct my own!

Believe in Jesus Christ

I came to Christ at age sixteen at the Liberty Theatre where I saw a Billy Graham film called *For Pete's Sake.* Prior to that time, I had only a vague idea about God. If you had asked me then if I believed in God, I would have said "yes." Attending a nearby church that reinforced Christian ideals, I thought of myself as a Christian. Though I had no idea what it meant to really be a believer in Christ, I remember playing a part in the Christmas play and attending a party for the youth group. Like many kids, I mostly remember sitting in a room full of tables as my mind wandered to think about many others things. Though I recall I did not like going to church, and didn't go much, I also remember feeling good about myself for having gone.

For many years, I did not understand what it meant to be a believer. I certainly never experienced God's presence, peace, leading, and power. I did not even know that such a thing was possible! That is, not until I heard the good news about Jesus Christ from Billy Graham through the movie entitled *For Pete's Sake*. At the time, I was attending Missouri Military Academy (MMA), a school I attended from eighth to twelfth grade. That day in the Liberty Theatre (I love that name), I understood for the first time that Jesus' death on the cross served as payment for all my sins. Jesus promised me forgiveness, and I chose to receive it: "This is My blood of the covenant, which is poured out for many for forgiveness of sins," He declared (Matthew 26:28). When I asked Jesus Christ to forgive me and to come into my life, something important happened to me at that moment. Yes, it was a private decision made in my heart and mind. But, when I left the Liberty Theatre, I walked back to the Academy with a new spring in my step. That day the grass appeared a deeper green, the sky shined a richer blue, and the birds sang more beautifully. Life brightened. I think I skipped a few times returning to campus. Why? I understood that Jesus promised me peace, and I received His peace: "These things I have spoken to you, so that in Me you may have peace" (John 16:33). He promised to help me, and I received His help. He said, "I will ask the Father, and He will give you another Helper, that He may be with you forever" (John 14:16). I felt hope. I felt that I found the purpose of life. I could tell, something just happened to me.

Obviously, I still struggled with issues teenagers commonly battle, but I cannot deny the peace and the presence that came to me on many occasions. As Peter said, I tasted of His kindness (1 Peter 2:3). My encounter with the Lord is captured in the old Scottish prayer that says, "Lord, I ain't what I'm gonna be. I ain't what I wanna be. But I ain't what I used to be." That pretty much sums up how I felt after my decision to believe in Jesus. Though a non-believer might chalk up my experience as mere psychological release or escape into a hopeful myth or fairy tale; I can only testify to what happened when I met Jesus personally.

The presence of divine power was evident in the events that followed. I am aware that some skeptics might refer to the experiences of Christians as mere coincidence. I contend that coincidence after coincidence is no longer coincidence. As God began to reveal Himself to me in practical ways, I felt like the early fisherman who followed Jesus. Though they had fished all night long without catching any fish, when Jesus said, "Put out into the deep water and let down your nets for a catch," Simon replied, "I will do as You say and let down the nets." The great quantity of fish they caught began to break their nets (Luke 5:4–6)! Someone on the shore might fairly exclaim, "Coincidence!" But, for these fishermen who knew their trade and experience, this experience was no coincidence!

Truly this is a "co-incidence," which I learned to call it from my friend Sam Ericsson, who I referenced earlier in this book, the lawyer who founded Advocates International. Sam often chatted about the co-incidents. He referred to them as God's incident meeting his incident as part of His-Story. He wrote me one time to tell me that he had 446 incidents recorded thus far. (He had a near photographic memory as a Harvard Law School graduate.) This was before the Lord called him home. He had stories like this, which was his first one:

> In August 1971 Bobby [his wife] and I had been married for six months. As I was mowing my lawn, a Grace Community Church pastor, Jerry Mitchell, pulled up in his Richard Petty blue Ford Pinto. He told me about a couple in our Sunday school class. The husband had lost his job and they were about to be evicted. I wrote a check for $235 to the GCC benevolence fund with instructions to tell the couple that friends in their class had given a gift. As Jerry drives away, the mailman arrives with the Saturday mail. Our Home Savings & Loan mortgage holder informed us that there was an adjustment to our escrow account for the mortgage, taxes, etc. of $20 per month less = $240 per year. I could still see Jerry's blue Pinto going down Hesby Street. That was the first time where I experienced the sowing and reaping principle firsthand and one of my earliest "co-incidents."

He also shared,

> In 1996, I was asked by New Tribes Missions to help them locate and hopefully free their three kidnapped missionaries in Colombia. To make a longer story short, I travelled to Stockholm and Oslo to meet with some Members of

Parliament that I had met—dramatically—at the National Prayer Breakfast in the USA. When I got to Oslo, I realized that I did not have the business card of the MP from Norway and no way to reach him nor could my office help because I had not stored his name in any traceable fashion. As I'm walking to the hotel from the train station in Oslo, I hear my name called by a guy who had just walked on by. It was the MP!

I loved Sam's stories, and there were 444 more! I also loved the story of Simon the fishermen because many things that skeptics would call coincidence appeared after I placed my faith in Jesus Christ. These experiences helped confirm to me the reality of Christ and His promises in my life. Though I cannot prove Christ's claims on the basis of my experience any more than these early fishermen could prove the deity of Jesus based on their nets full of fish, I can tell you that good things—God things—started taking place. And, they started taking place in my own family.

One of the great "coincidences" is that my whole family came to believe in Jesus Christ shortly after my own decision to do so. When my mother saw something taking place in me because of my faith in Jesus and my study of the Bible, she joined a Bible study at a conservative church. There, for the first time, she realized what it meant to have a personal relationship with Jesus Christ. Though Mom had gone over the years to a liberal church on Christmas and Easter, she had never personally placed her faith in Jesus Christ. When Helen Modjeska, one of the leaders of the Bible study, recognized this, she took Mom aside and asked, "Jay, have you ever received Jesus Christ into your life?"

My mother said, "No one ever asked me that question before."

Helen pursued, "Jay, would you like to receive Jesus Christ into your life?" My mother said, "Well, I guess it wouldn't hurt."

Mom prayed to receive Jesus Christ because she understood that God loved her and sent Christ to die on the cross for her sins. Once Mom acknowledged that she was a sinner and needed forgiveness, she asked Christ to take up residence within her.

Soon after my mom received Jesus Christ into her life at age fifty-three, she came to me with tears rolling down her cheeks. In dismay she said, "All my life the way to know Christ personally was right here in the Bible, and I never saw it before, and no one ever told me about it."

My mom had a revolutionary encounter with Jesus Christ. She could not withhold this information from my sister, who prayed to receive Jesus Christ shortly after that. Then, my brother-in-law, a professor, saw the change in my sister, and he prayed to receive Jesus Christ into his life. Eventually, my dad came to Jesus Christ. All four of these individuals came to Jesus Christ within a twelve-month period, which was my freshman year at Wheaton College.

My mom's experience with her newfound faith led her to begin speaking at the Christian women's club. Because she had lived fifty-three years before knowing Christ personally, she testified to the difference between her "before-Christ life and her after-Christ experience." Once she became a child of God and began an intimate relationship with Abba Father, she began to know, like the early disciples, the "odd coincidences" of full fishing nets. Having obeyed the universal will of God to believe, she began experiencing the unique will of God in the details of her life. And let me add, my dad changed. He faithfully attended church and would sit in his chair at home and sing the old hymns. In addition, he was burdened for his brother's salvation, my uncle Andy. Dad longed for me to talk to him, along with other friends, all of whom prayed to receive Christ. As for my uncle, he lived two more years after he received Christ and his life radically changed in that twenty-four-month period. At his funeral a woman who knew my uncle for half a century said, "When he received Christ, he totally changed." As for my dad, he could not contain the joy he felt over his brother and the others who came to Christ, doing so because they observed my dad's change. Mom and Dad are now in heaven, and we deeply miss them but rejoice they are with Christ. As for my sister Ann and brother-in-law Fred, they have faithfully followed Christ and served Him in the local church for nearly fifty years. As a family, something happened to us, and it was good.

Looking back on my decision at the Liberty Theatre to *believe* in Christ as my Savior and make Him the Lord of my life, I am awed now to see how that decision set the course for the rest of my life. My hunger to know more of the Word of God first led to my studies at Wheaton College and the privilege of mentorship there by seasoned men and women of God. The counsel of some of these leaders then pointed me toward training experiences in church work, community counseling, and seminary. When I now consider the joy that Sarah and I experience as God's servants working to improve marriages, I am awed at how this work really began at the Liberty Theatre the day I chose to believe in Christ. Though the journey we have shared has had tough stretches, the decision to obey the first will of God (John 6:40) to *believe* in Christ was the first step to experiencing God's unfolding goodness to me and my family. I could never have imagined in 1967 how my personal decision to follow Christ would spiral out into the public ministry that Sarah and I now share.

Give Thanks in Everything

When we get home to be with our Father in heaven, I believe the words, "Thank You, Lord," will be at the heart of all that we do and say. But, to be honest, most of us spend a lot of time here grumbling about something. I am no different.

Growing up, I had no idea about the importance of giving thanks in all things. Oh, sure, I knew about Thanksgiving. In November, I could express gratefulness for what I possessed, especially the turkey drumsticks; but I knew nothing about giving thanks in the midst of difficulties. Expressions of anger came far more naturally. As a young boy, I frequently threw temper tantrums at home. I remember Mom saying to me, "Everybody at school says you are such a wonderful boy, so why don't you act that way at home?" I wanted to, but I guess home was the place where I could kick the wall.

Later, when I attended military school, I also had a few moments of intense anger. Once, while walking between classes, I scuffed my spit-shine shoe. As I spewed out my anger, from behind me, I felt a hand rest on my shoulder and then heard the voice of the commandant, "Calm down, Mr. Eggerichs, calm down." Another time the barber cut my hair too short, which to this day I don't understand why that bothered me since we all had short haircuts. Even so, I returned to my room blistering mad. My cool, calm, and collected roommate looked at me like I came off a psych ward and said with a measure of disgust, "It'll grow back, for heaven's sake."

These were small things. I did have some big problems, too. But, in those days, I never considered giving thanks to God for little or large difficulties. Though I praised God when I prayed with others, I cannot remember the first time I decided to give thanks on the heels of a problem. The importance of this practice became clear to me during a short season between college and graduate school when I spent time reading Christian biographies. The power of praise in the lives of men such as Hudson Taylor, Adoniram Judson, Jim Elliot, William Carey, Martin Luther, George Mueller, and many others really moved me. As I read their life stories and learned of the severe setbacks that shattered their hopes, I learned how each one exercised an optimistic faith in spite of severe setbacks. They gave thanks to God ahead of time and in the face of what seemed insurmountable odds. They thanked God not because they expected Him to miraculously change the circumstances, but because He would powerfully use the events for a greater good. I would say to myself, "Why get so angry when you should give thanks? After all, God is in control, and you aren't dying for your faith. This matter isn't that big of a deal. Good will grow back into your life. 'Calm down, Mr. Eggerichs, calm down.'"

Certainly after marriage, Sarah influenced me in the giving of thanks. She loves to give thanks and would often ask me, "Have you given thanks?" Though I counseled people to give thanks in their difficulties, I also struggled to be grateful for things that came my way. Some of the greatest challenges to a thankful heart came through issues related to church decisions. When, for instance, heated attacks against me erupted in response to the need to relocate the church, let a staff member go, or start a new program, I recoiled in disbelief. Could I be grateful for ungrateful people? Could I give thanks to God for people who did not thank God for me?

I know that giving thanks does not mean we must feel immediately grateful. Sometimes we feel kicked in the gut, and rebounding takes weeks if not months. People do or say things that leave us gasping, and we need time to fill our lungs before we can breathe normally. But, if we put our heads in the right direction and determine to give thanks, we will eventually end up seeing God's grace in the events.

I remember one time that the ability to give thanks took me a while. Church pressures had pushed me to such a breaking point that the board decided to give me some time away with another one of the pastors. After walking, talking, and praying with my pastor friend and resting at my mom's house in Florida, I was able to regain my spiritual equilibrium. Eventually, I was able to stop my mind from racing around the well-beaten track of "who said what and why, and what right did they have to voice those things." With the help of my friend, I pushed through the pain to find peace in praising God and giving thanks. Where might I be if I had not been encouraged to give thanks in this moment of pain? Rather than mirror the spirit of Job's wife who said, "Curse God and die," my friend stayed by me until I could give thanks as Job eventually did.

Through the years as Sarah and I have prayed as a couple, the major attitude we seek to express in prayer is one of thanksgiving. When we ask God for specific things, we thank Him that He can do them. We thank Him for what He wills to happen. We thank Him that He cares more than we care. We thank Him for allowing this situation to cause us to depend on Him. We have learned—and are learning—that when we want to give thanks, we learn a multitude of ways to give thanks. Think about it. We can thank Him for the past. We can thank Him for the present. We can thank Him for the future. We can also thank Him for all the ways He has loved and accepted us while we have been growing in His image.

Submit in Doing Right

One of the ways I can be thankful for God's fatherly love of me concerns this area of submission. I was not born with a retiring personality: I needed to learn submission. Angry temper tantrums and clenched fists surfaced easily in my childhood. As I observed my dad's acts of rage toward my mom, I would lose control. At age ten or thereabouts, I picked up a butcher knife and told my mom that I intended to stab Dad. Though I had no intention of doing what I threatened, my outburst accurately reflects the mixture of anger, helplessness, and need for control that dominated my response to the dysfunctional authority structure in my home at that juncture.

God didn't waste any time with me getting to the point on this issue. I was sent to military school in the eighth grade. At an age when many teens are testing the waters by rebelling against authority figures, I was forced to obey uncompromising authority figures. Years later I realized that if I had not gone to military school, serious problems could have developed in my home. What would I have done as a seventeen-year-old boy when Dad went into a fit of rage against Mom? I shudder to think that I might have turned dangerously violent toward my dad if I had not learned how to respect and submit to authority.

God in His grace saw this trait unfolding and knew I needed correction. Interestingly, I learned years later that when Mom decided to send me to military school, she did not know how she would pay for it. She loved to tell the story of how God (what she felt she knew about Him) met that need one day when she went to the post office to mail some packages. Deep in thought about how she would fund my attendance at private military school, she just so happened to run into her insurance agent. When he asked her how she was doing, she shared, "I'm wondering how I can pay for Eddie to go to military school." He replied, "That's easy. You can borrow against your insurance policy." Though this event took place six years before she received Jesus Christ in her life, Mom felt at that moment that God Himself reached down and took care of the burden of her heart. She sensed it was God, and said so, though she did not know the Lord personally, and said years later that God in His kindness helped her, which is one of the factors that opened her heart to learning more about a personal relationship with Christ. From my standpoint, I truly believe He did move that day. He knew my future. I needed to go to military school for a variety of reasons. I needed distance from my dad as I entered my middle teen years; and my parents needed time to deal with their own difficulties without the complications of my adolescent struggles. Most importantly, though, I needed to learn how to respect and submit to authority figures. Though there were countless times when I did not like military school, for some strange reason, I wanted to stay, and did for five years.

As I look back, I see a direct correlation between learning to submit to human authority and my encounter with God. I can now see that opening my heart to Jesus Christ and His lordship was made easier as I practiced submission to human authority. In learning to respectfully do what was rightfully required of me when I didn't want to do it, I learned principles that continue to aid my walk with the Lord. I recognize there is a cost in following the Lord, but I am less afraid of that than I would have been had I not attended a school with authority figures all over the place. Sadly, some people never experience the unique will and leading of Jesus Christ because they do not submit to Him, and they do not submit to Him because they have not submitted to human authority.

Today, I do not view submission to authority as a bad thing, though there are countries where this is a major burden of mine. I just learned that the Chinese authorities mandated that Christian parents cannot take their children to church. This is evil and heartbreaking. However, with most of us, Romans 13 still applies.

But closer to home is Hebrews 13:17. This is church leadership. We read, "Obey your leaders and submit to them, for they keep watch over your souls" (Hebrews 13:17). For me, good things come when obeying this instruction, and most of us need to recognize the importance of this for us. Three major events in my life confirm to me the powerful leading of God because I submitted to godly, wise church authority.

The first occurred in 1980 when I was interviewing for the position of senior pastor of Trinity Church in East Lansing. Since I had been ordained to the ministry by the pastoral staff at Grace Community Church in Sun Valley, California, the leadership there supported me by sending two elders, Ralph Wong and Paul Guay, to meet with the elders at Trinity to help discern if it would be a good match. Considering the trade of sunny California for Michigan winters, I was tempted to call this a "wong guay" flight from California to Michigan! But, I was honored by the love and wise partnership of these men in my decision-making process.

Why did Grace send these two elders? The Grace board said to the Trinity board, if God is not in this, we want to protect Trinity from Emerson and Emerson from Trinity. From this unprecedented umbrella of protection and direction, these two elders negotiated with the elders of Trinity concerning the philosophy of ministry they believed God had called me to fulfill. They did not want me to accept a call from a church at odds with this philosophy. After several hours of discussing my job description, a meeting that excluded me, I remember Paul Guay coming out of the meeting to tell me to accept the call, which I did. Because I had so thoroughly entrusted myself to Ralph and him, only later did I think to ask, "Oh, by the way, what am I getting paid?" I knew that the authority of these godly, wise men would guard and guide me. It did! My submission to them and the elders at Trinity resulted in a ministry experience that brought me much joy.

Let me add one other thing I learned about submission while at Grace Community Church. Sam Ericsson, serving then as the church administrator, told me that one of the reasons the elders called me into the pastoral ministry had to do with my copy machine duties. When I first came to Grace Church, I served as the security guard, which allowed me to study late in the evening. During those night shifts, Sam asked me to run off copies of teaching materials for some of the pastors. I did that gladly, running off thousands of sets of curriculum. I also did this because Sam himself demonstrated humble service and a submissive attitude toward authority. Though I had no idea at the time that Sam was a Harvard Law grad who could have made ten times what he was making at Grace, I was still awed by the way he served without arrogance. Modeling his servant posture, I learned how submission to humble tasks shapes us, as well as furthers the kingdom. Little did I know at the time, however, that the elders would later determine my qualification for pastoral ministry based on my submission to do this menial task! They concluded because I was willing to respectfully serve in this low capacity, doing what was required, I would serve well as a pastor.

Much later in my career, many years into my service as senior pastor at Trinity, I experienced another situation in which submission to authority worked for my good. At the time I had been seriously exploring co-laboring with Dr. Ken Canfield at the National Institute of Fathering in Manhattan, Kansas. Feeling drawn to the work being done there, I decided to resign from Trinity and head out to Kansas. The church board, however, informed me that they wanted to do what Grace Church had done years earlier. So, they sent two board members to Kansas to explore the opportunity. When they returned, the board said, "You can do here what you want to do there." They then created a win-win arrangement. Wow, submission worked to my advantage! Then in 1998 God unfolded to me the principles related to the Love and Respect marriage material that Sarah and I now teach across the country. At that time, I became vividly aware of how the material could vitally help couples. Nevertheless, I knew that I could not shepherd a large congregation while simultaneously presenting conferences on weekends and developing program resources. This time when I submitted my dilemma to the board, they came to an amazing conclusion. After much prayer and discussion about the unique ability of the Love and Respect message to address a huge need in the culture, they said, "We want to pay you full-time for nine months to help you launch this ministry." Wow! Authority figures can operate to our benefit!

Does submission to authority always work out like this? In the long run, yes. In the short run, not always. The three examples I have just shared involved submission to godly men. The fruit of obeying their counsel was immediate. In some circumstances, the benefit of submission is not always immediately clear. One of my most difficult experiences of submitting to authority happened early in my career. It is only in hindsight that I can see God's favor working itself out through my submission. Now, I can clearly give thanks for what God taught me through this experience!

Years ago as a twenty-four-year-old, I was an assistant pastor in a Midwestern church. One of my numerous assignments involved preaching once a month. When overflow crowds forced ushers to open sliding doors the second and third time I preached, the pastor no longer wanted me to preach on Sunday morning. Since it had appeared to go well, I was surprised; but I accepted his decision without complaint. Nine months later the senior pastor orchestrated my release by informing several board members that our relationship did not jive. This time I was stunned. When I inquired for specifics, this pastor told me in front of three board members that I did things such as sit down on the platform before he sat down. In disbelief, I said, "I had no idea. I did not do that out of disrespect. Had you told me, I would have stood and waited for you to sit down." Nothing I said satisfied that committee of four. When I asked, "Do you three wonder why the relationship is not working out?" they declined to get into the details. They reassured me that I was young and would get over this situation and have a bright future ahead of me.

Disheartened by the interaction between me and the authority figures in this first church experience, I wrestled in prayer about what to do next. While I would have liked to have been guided by the kind of counsel I later found at Grace, God did not desert me in this crisis. When I resigned as they requested, I joined with another pastor friend, Larry Johnson, to launch The Open Door Christian Counseling Center. We based this new counseling ministry on the principles of George Mueller, who trusted in God alone to supply the needs of his orphanage. Mirroring his practice of faith, we decided to not charge for our counseling, solicit donations from the business community, or make our financial needs known. As best as we knew how, we would live by faith, looking solely to God for these resources. Time and time again during Larry's and my time at Open Door, God taught me principles of faith as it pertains to relying on Him to provide for every financial need that I might not have learned so quickly if I'd depended on established structures.

During our first year, 1975, we established the budget at $30,000. Like clockwork, every two weeks for that whole year, the finances rolled in according to budget: To God be the glory! The second year we established the budget at $36,000 and like clockwork, every two weeks, the finances rolled in—until April!

At that point the money slowed down, putting us in a $700 deficit. On an April day, late in the afternoon, Larry and I met at the office to discuss our financial dilemma. I remember feeling angry over the shortfall, thinking the critics of our faith-venture would relish the news of our failing. However, I soon confessed my anxiety and ungratefulness in the face of God's miraculous provision over the previous sixteen months. Together we acknowledged before God His promise to meet our needs, and we thanked Him for hearing our request about the $700. We also told the Lord we knew that He had not promised to meet our budget, only our needs. As we would tell others, "We may need protein, and pray for a filet mignon, but we may only get peanut butter." We ended the day by thanking God for supporting us as He deemed appropriate. The next day back at the office Larry said, "Do you remember that schoolteacher with four children who recently got divorced, the one I led to Christ?" I replied, "Yes."

"Well," said Larry, "the other day she asked if we took donations, and I told her that we did; but I gave it no further thought. Last night she knocked on our door and handed me a check for $600!" In 1975 most single parents did not dole out that kind of money! We rejoiced and thanked God in prayer. We had $600 of the $700 needed. With our faith bolstered, we asked God to bring in the additional $100.

Shortly thereafter I went to the mailbox and returned with an unmarked, unsealed envelope containing four $20 bills and a $10 bill, totaling $90 in cash. Unbelievable!

At that point, with the $690, we knew God would provide the final $10. Later we heard a knock at the door. As we opened it, there stood a little old lady who identified herself as a retired schoolteacher from the Cedar Rapids school district who now lived in Sun City, Arizona. Returning to Cedar Rapids to visit some of her girlfriends, she read in the *Cedar Rapids Gazette* about the Open Door Counseling Center. Recently, the newspaper highlighted the ministry, but the paper had said nothing about giving donations. She asked, "Do you boys take donations?" We said, "Yes." So, she wrote out a check, and sure enough she handed us a check for $10.

God supplied the $700! We grinned from ear to ear. Did I feel a little sheepish for my previous anger and lack of belief that God could pull us through? You bet. But, I also got a great lesson about who is really in charge and what happens when we respond in thankful submission to Him. Then, to top it off, we enjoyed one more blessing as a result of this crisis. Because of the sweetness of this little lady, we decided—contrary to our principle of not telling—to inform her of the three events, the $600, the $90, and then her $10.

She replied, "Boys, that's strange. I am on a fixed income, but each month I set aside $5, above my tithe, for organizations like yours. Each month I love to find a ministry like this and give my little five dollars. As I drove over here today the Lord spoke to my heart saying, "Double it." All of us stood in amazement!

Did God remove me from that Midwestern church just so He could teach me lessons on faith? I don't know. But, when we follow the commands of the four wills, we are positioned to experience God's power. Sometimes God does "big" things quickly through unlikely means—such as meeting the budget through the big and small gifts of people of faith. Other times, it may take years to see the plan that God was weaving through our difficult times. If, however, we stay faithful to following those things that Scriptures tell us are "the will of God," we will reap good in the end.

Abstain from Sexual Sin

Looking back I now marvel at the goodness of God in orchestrating the events of my early life in a way that focused the principles of the Love and Respect seminar we now present. Growing up during the sexual revolution of the 1960s, I was immersed in culture that was throwing out traditional values and advocating sexual freedom. Sexual purity, a fundamental way to demonstrate love and respect to God and one's spouse, was hardly the message of the era. But, where did my wise and loving heavenly Father place me during all this? At a military school! Missouri Military Academy (MMA) in

Mexico, Missouri. For a few years, God sheltered me from the secular culture of public high school with all the temptations of girls, alcohol, and drugs.

It did not hit me until years later how fortunate I was to live a cloistered life of sorts for this season of my life. I have no idea what I might have done without this protection. Though I realize military school might well be the place of temptation for some, for me it was a protection. I have often wondered what I would have done each weekend in a public high school. At MMA every weekend I had to clean, undergo inspections, participate in sports, march to church, participate in a parade, attend Vespers, and go to bed at 9:45 p.m. Obviously this regimen reduced my exposure to parties with women, alcohol, and drugs. I realize that some teens navigate this passage in a God-honoring way, but the circumstances of my home life at that stage might have put me at risk. My heart goes out to all those who have had to wrestle with these temptations while negotiating the development of their own identities.

God protected me once again from being on the frontlines of the sexual revolution of the '70s by allowing me to attend Wheaton College, a Christian school outside Chicago. Mature friends and believers there who advocated God's view of sexual purity helped restrain me from indulging my sensual appetites. Of course, I could have gotten sexually involved there, just as I might have at military school. But, the point is, the Wheaton environment honored sexual abstinence, and God used that to help protect me. This is one reason why I see the benefits of a restrictive environment. These settings protect us from the pull of sexual exploration that resides in us.

What I learned from my experiences at MMA and Wheaton has helped me over the years of my ministry. This is it: temptations limit themselves when we have guardrails. Those guardrails are not restrictive, but protective. We put them up to keep our toddlers from falling down steps. The state puts them up on winding, mountainous roads to keep vehicles from reeling over cliffs. Guardrails prevent us from going head-over-heels into sin. You only find them in places where it's easy to fall. Sex is one of those places. Since sexual temptations don't evaporate after marriage, I have been grateful for what I learned at Wheaton and MMA about the importance of putting guardrails between me and the seducing influence. Now that the culture I live in doesn't do it for me, I find ways to construct my own defenses in places where I know I am vulnerable. This practice has proved invaluable. As a pastor, I knew that abstaining from sexual sin ranked top on God's priority list for me if I were to experience His unique leading in my life. I recall hearing people say that power, money, and sex are the downfall of men. For most pastors, power and money are not the driving forces. That left sex as the culprit for most pastors. I knew in my twenties, thirties, forties, fifties, and beyond that sexual temptations would confront me if I traveled alone.

I did not have the assurance that I would do any better resisting this temptation than many men do whose jobs require them to travel routinely. I feared my vulnerability, and I feared God. Therefore, I rarely traveled. At the same time, I longed for God to uniquely lead and use me beyond the local church. For years, I felt trapped. I told Sarah, "I feel like there is a lid on my ministry." But, since we knew why, we relinquished this to God, trusting He would honor us. He did. Today, our children are grown, and Sarah now travels with me in the ministry. What the Lord is doing through our Love and Respect ministry blesses us beyond what we deserve! As "empty-nesters," we can enjoy this season without compromising care to our children or risking the sexual temptations that confront those who travel alone. Sarah and I are glad we waited to travel together. Paul addresses this concern in 1 Corinthians 9:5, "Do we not have a right to take along a believing wife, even as the rest of the apostles and the brothers of the Lord and Cephas?" Because the wives and apostles Paul refers to in this passage did not have children at home, they were, therefore, free to travel together. I believe young pastors would do well to remember this. We have lost common sense today!

But, you might argue, you don't have to travel to face sexual temptation. What about the Internet? You are right to assume this is the easiest way to fall prey to sexual immorality. I tell people that everything we do on the Internet is being stored somewhere. There is a digital footprint of our activity. For this reason, a person must not foolishly conclude they can stay in the dark on this, and even if one can stay in the dark, God sees all. One forfeits God's joyful presence, empowering hand, and personal leading. Is it worth it?

Each person must do whatever is necessary to stay in the light. God expects this. And, as we have stated: "Observed behavior changes." The inverse is also true: Unobserved addictions remain, until they are exposed; that what they thought was a well-kept secret is out in the open to their utter humiliation.

However, when something is brought into the light, the pull of that temptation subsides. I knew that God could do great things through those who kept sexually pure, and I heard Him saying to me what I share with many men and women on this topic, "We are going to the mat on this sex issue, and no holds barred. You must cry 'Uncle,' giving in, giving up, and giving way to me. As a man of honor, honor me now, and watch what is about to happen."

Let me close by saying that Jesus sent the Holy Spirit to help me out of the temptation of sexual sin, and He will help you too. What comfort and hope this brings. God promises: "No temptation has overtaken you but such as is common to man; and God is faithful, who will not allow you to be tempted beyond what you are able, but with the temptation will provide the way of escape also, so that you will be able to endure it" (1 Corinthians 10:13). Talk about personal attention! When I want out of temptation, God will help me find a way out. Almighty God will enter my situation and point to an exit sign. If only each of us could see all the ways God has protected us during our temptations! Sometimes I envision standing before the Lord and having Him replay the dramatic ways of escape He provided for me. I wanted His power in ministry, His wisdom during trials, His leading concerning new opportunities, His guidance concerning marriage, and the list goes on. But, in the end, He will say, "Emerson, I understand all of these things, but where I showed up most often was during your temptations." Thank You, Lord!

Final Word: Ask the Helper for Help!

Though God commands us to believe, abstain, give thanks, and submit (B.A.G.S.), our inner posture can be dependent on Him as we pray, "Lord, You know my heart. I need help to trust You when You seem silent, walk in moral purity when temptations are real, give thanks when I am angry at what happened, and submit in doing right when it feels too demanding and unfair."

You and I need God's help in following these four universal wills, and He expects us to realize that's okay. This is why God sent us His Holy Spirit and He refers to him as the Helper. He is the helper because I need help.

An obvious point like this must not escape our notice; it must comfort our hearts. What a joy to read passages like these:

> Hebrews 4:16: "Therefore let us draw near with confidence to the throne of grace, so that we may receive mercy and find grace to help in time of need."

> Hebrews 13:6: "So that we confidently say, 'The Lord is my helper, I will not be afraid. What will man do to me?'"

Concerning **believing** in Jesus Christ, who among us has not wondered if we have enough faith to trust the Lord when life circumstances overwhelm us? Will we shut down and stop believing? Or, will we echo the man who said to Jesus, "Lord, I believe. Help my unbelief"? That has been my prayer on many occasions, and it is a sacred thing to ask for help from the Helper and our loving Lord. The apostles themselves "said to the Lord, 'Increase our faith!'" (Luke 17:5).

Concerning **giving thanks** in everything, who among us always wants to give thanks in the midst of trials? None of us. Consequently, there come these moments when we can give voice to God about our desire for Him to help us in such a way that we are motivated to give thanks. A prayer of the Israelites was, "Save us, O God of our salvation, and gather us and deliver us . . . to give thanks to Your holy name" (1 Chronicles 16:35; Psalm 106:47). It is okay to parrot from the heart this petition, "Bring my soul out of prison, So that I may give thanks to Your name" (Psalm 142:7). We can humbly ask God to orchestrate life events in such a way that it frees us up to give thanks. Psalm 42:5 says, "Hope in God, for I shall again praise Him for the help of His presence." We must anticipate His helpful presence and let that ignite the giving of thanks. Another helpful prayer is, "God, 'sustain me with a willing spirit' (Psalm 51:12) to give thanks."

Romans 8:7 states the carnal "mind . . . does not subject itself to the law of God, for it is not even able to do so." Our sinful nature rebels against any kind of submission when it counters our self-serving desires and goals. So, concerning **submitting** in doing right, who among us wants to defer to those in authority over us who are requiring us to do appropriate tasks when we prefer not to do these assignments? During such requests, the cry of our heart must be, "Jesus, everything in me wants to rebel against this boss making me do something I don't want to do, particularly when I feel it is unfair to me. But because this request is not evil, help me to be deferential. Help me to serve as You serve. Help me to realize that this is part of the molding process within my own soul so that I learn better to submit to You. Oh, Holy Spirit, help me to submit. Help me counter my carnal nature that can so quickly turn ugly."

Concerning **abstaining** from sexual sin, who among us does not experience temptations? Jesus Himself was tempted and had to deal with these temptations. None of us will escape these enticements that come from within and without. I find myself often praying a portion of the Lord's Prayer. "Oh God through Jesus Christ have mercy on me a sinner. 'Lead me not into temptation but deliver me from this evil.'" Temptation can be a daily thing. I wish this weren't true but it is. We live in a fallen world and the devil is real and so is our flesh. Daily, we need God's help. Ultimately, we must acknowledge our weaknesses and accept the reality of temptation and that we must struggle in keeping our eyes fixed on Jesus. Some think that because the struggle is constant, that the Christian life doesn't work for them and that God has no intentions of helping them. That's untrue. What is true is that the struggle is always greater than we desire. Yet, it is never so great that we cannot eventually triumph over these temptations. The Word of God always promises a way of escape if we want to exit that hallway (1 Corinthians 10:13).

In all of these situations, we must never let defeat, defeat us. We must get back up in the ring of life. We must stay in the fight. We have the Father, Son, and Holy Spirit to help us.

We must continue to turn to God for help, and that's okay to do.

ACKNOWLEDGMENTS

Special thanks to Devin Maddox of B&H Publishing for his editorial input in refining the content of this manuscript and for his conviction that the message of this book needed to be available to the body of Christ around the world. His application of this message to people in his world turning to him for counsel blessed my heart.

I also wish to thank Gail Eubanks who helped edit earlier portions of this book, and more recently Kevin Harvey. Their input was most helpful and I am grateful.

And, a heartfelt acknowledgment to Sarah, my wife, who prayed for me while writing this book and contributed to the content of this book by living the four wills, as I describe in this book.

ABOUT THE AUTHOR

Emerson Eggerichs, PhD, completed his studies in child and family ecology at Michigan State University and is the author of the *New York Times* bestseller *Love & Respect*. He and his wife, Sarah, present to live audiences around the country in their Love and Respect Conferences. As a communication expert, Emerson has also spoken to groups from the NFL, NBA, PGA, the Navy SEALs, and members of Congress.

Emerson was the senior pastor of Trinity Church in Lansing, Michigan, for almost twenty years. He holds a BA in biblical studies from Wheaton College, an MA in communication from Wheaton College Graduate School, and an MDiv from the University of Dubuque Theological Seminary. He and Sarah have been married since 1973 and have three adult children.

NOTES

Chapter 2

1. https://www.health.harvard.edu/blog/first-do-no-harm-201510138421.

2. The ethics of end-of-life decision-making is incredibly fraught. To be clear, God loves life and hates death. We, in no way, intend to mean that euthanasia could "seem" good, but rather intend with this hypothetical situation to illustrate that keeping the grandfather on life support systems would not allow him to die of natural causes. For instance, a person can be brain dead but medical technology can keep the person alive who otherwise would die of natural causes. Such situations pain every family member. Though family members never want to be put in a position to allow a beloved grandfather to die, that decision differs from injecting him with drugs to end his life.

3. http://www.navigators.org/us/ministries/college/daily-devo?pg_mon=4&pg_day=18.

Chapter 3

1. Bernhard Langer, *Bernhard Langer: My Autobiography* (London: Hodder & Stoughton, 2002), 50.

2. Ibid., 51.

3. Ibid.

Chapter 4

1. Words from an eighteenth-century woman, quoted by Mary Tileston in *Daily Strength of Daily Needs* (Springdale, PA: Whitaker House, 1997), 21.

Chapter 5

1. Suicide is a serious matter, one with which pastors and counselors must treat with the utmost responsibility. When concern about someone's intention to harm themselves enters the picture, the proper authorities and procedures must be pursued to ensure the safety of everyone. Every church, counseling group, and Christian ministry should have a plan in place for how to engage suicide. For me personally, I would not have said what Merlin said about giving thanks for suicide per se. I would have counseled, "Have you given thanks to God for these stressful circumstances, that leave you feeling hopeless and abandoned, with the view that God is loving and sovereign and that with your humble

giving of thanks you allow God to respond to you personally in this time of despair? Are you willing to give thanks as a way of saying to God that you trust Him though you feel your situation is impossible for Him to change or provide you with a peace that passes all understanding in the midst of this depression? Are you willing to act on 1 Thessalonians 5:18? I hope this actually stirs your heart just a bit with the possibility that He will lovingly surprise you."

Chapter 6

1. Corrie Ten Boom, *Clippings from My Notebook* (Nashville, TN: Thomas Nelson, 1982), 56.

2. Ibid., 57.

Chapter 7

1. Story shared personally with the author.

2. The wife gave permission to use this story of submission.

Chapter 8

1. This oft-quoted English translation of Bonhoeffer's original writing can be found in the foreword of his *The Cost of Discipleship* (London: SCM Press Ltd., 1959; repr. New York: Touchstone, 1995), 11.

2. https://qz.com/900567/us-supreme-court-nominee-neil-gorsuchs-controversial-hobby-lobby-decision-explained/.

3. J. Vernon McGee, *First Peter,* Through the Bible Commentary Series (Nashville, TN: Thomas Nelson Publishers, 1991), 58.

Chapter 9

1. Mark Regnerus, *Cheap Sex: The Transformation of Men, Marriage, and Monogamy* (New York: Oxford University Press, 2017), 187.

2. John Stonestreet and G. Shane Morris, "Only in the Lord: Dating Unbelievers Deadens Faith," *Breakpoint* (9/13/17); http://breakpoint.org/2017/09/breakpoint-only-in-the-lord/.

3. http://www.physiciansforlife.org/cohabitation-vs-marriage-26-research-findings/.

4. C. S. Lewis, *Mere Christianity* (1952; repr. Grand Rapids, MI: Zondervan, 2001), 142.

5. Drs. Joe S. McIlhaney and Freda McKissic Bush, "Hooked: The Bonding Power of Sex," *Family Life*; see http://www.familylife.com/articles/topics/parenting/challenges/sexual-purity/hooked-the-bonding-power-of-sex.

Chapter 10

1. http://treesachen.blogspot.com/2008/09/fantasy-versus-reality.html.

2. Joseph Thayer, *Thayer's Greek-English Lexicon of the New Testament* (Peabody, MA: Hendrickson Publishers, 1996), *pornia*.

3. C. S. Lewis, *The Collected Letters of C. S. Lewis Volume II* (New York: HarperCollins, 2004), 507.